Know-It-All

Wine

Know-It-All
Wine

The 50 Essential Topics,
Each Explained in Under a Minute >

Editor **Gérard Basset** OBE
Foreword **Annette Alvarez-Peters**

Contributors

Gérard Basset OBE
David Bird MW
Martin Campion
Jeremy Dixon
Paul Lukacs
Debra Meiburg MW
Jane Parkinson
Stephen Skelton MW

WELLFLEET
P R E S S

Brimming with creative inspiration, how-to projects, and useful information to enrich your everyday life, Quarto Knows is a favorite destination for those pursuing their interests and passions. Visit our site and dig deeper with our books into your area of interest: Quarto Creates, Quarto Cooks, Quarto Homes, Quarto Lives, Quarto Drives, Quarto Explores, Quarto Gifts, or Quarto Kids.

This book was conceived, designed, and produced by
Ivy Press
An imprint of The Quarto Group
The Old Brewery, 6 Blundell Street
London N7 9BH, United Kingdom
T (0)20 7700 6700 **F** (0)20 7700 8066

Creative Director **Peter Bridgewater**
Publisher **Susan Kelly**
Editorial Director **Tom Kitch**
Art Director **Michael Whitehead**
Commissioning Editor **Stephanie Evans**
Project Editor **Jamie Pumfrey**
Designer **Ginny Zeal**
Illustrator **Ivan Hissey**
Profiles & Glossaries Text **Jeremy Dixon**

Printed in China

MIX
Paper from
responsible sources
FSC® C001701

CONTENTS

FOREWORD
Annette Alvarez-Peters

My journey to the world of wine began twenty
years ago, when I was appointed to a beverage alcohol buyer position.
Although I was an experienced merchant, I had limited wine knowledge and
was facing an enormous learning curve. Determined to learn all that I could,
I was astonished at the range, and depth, of the many variables of the wine
industry. I not only needed to learn the business overall, but also the
important details surrounding soil, viticulture, vinification, grape varieties,
and the regions they reside, and a host of other fascinating disciplines.

In my early days as a buyer, I reached out to as many individuals as
possible in an effort to learn the business. The volume of information was
overwhelming, and I needed to become a sponge to absorb the knowledge
available to me. I read numerous wine books and all the relevant trade
publications. I attended all kinds of trade tastings, harvest festivals, and

visited many wineries. More importantly, I asked a million questions—from the most elementary to the most insightful.

Throughout my travels, I've had the privilege of meeting producers both big and small. Clearly, the common thread among them is to produce the highest quality wine possible given the incredible diversity of their vineyards. As impressive, and educational, that these diverse wine properties can be, it's the families and individuals that care for the land that are most extraordinary. I am grateful to have toured vineyards and cellars and tasted wines with some of the most notable producers, such as Robert Mondavi to Christian Moueix to Marchesi Piero Antinori. I have grown from their generosity in sharing their knowledge and passion for wine.

Some of the best resources in my learning curve have been some of the most accomplished and knowledgeable Masters: Masters of Wine and Master Sommeliers. These Masters have spent years studying every facet of the wine business from regions, soil, farming practices, and grape varieties to the foundations of retail and restaurant success. The Masters' abilities to taste and evaluate wines are nearly supernatural. Gérard Basset is only one of four individuals, worldwide, to be a Double Master, having earned both Master of Wine and Master Sommelier. Simply put, I was thrilled the day I met Gerard. He is both brilliant and entertaining and exceedingly generous in sharing the wealth of his knowledge of wine.

As a purchaser for a large retailer, I have the utmost appreciation for consumers. A very important part of my wine journey has been observing and learning about consumer behavior. What influences their wine buying decisions? What do they like to drink? How much are they willing to explore? Today, consumers are rewarded with quality wines in every price range. Furthermore, technology has provided unprecedented access to information about wines from the world over, and wine lovers have never had better tools to enhance their knowledge.

This book is a perfect tool to help build knowledge and to discover your passion for wine. To your health!

INTRODUCTION

Gérard Basset OBE

Wine has a long, rich, and truly fascinating history.
This remarkable beverage has quenched our thirst, heightened our passions, and loosened our tongues ever since people in ancient Mesopotamia—or perhaps even before—first trod grapes and drank this elixir. Wine is the drink of conviviality, of celebrations, of success, and of gatherings great and small; wine is sensual and sensorial. But why should the soil in a vineyard plot mean so much to the contents of our glass? What alchemy turns this juice from the humble fruit of the vine into a drink capable of being cellared for decades? While wine generates much interest, the myriad grape varieties and wine styles can be bewildering and the language of wine can seem mysterious, too.

This book decants the subject, revealing the art and the science behind crus and clos, racking and riddling, and providing important insights into Burgundy, Bordeaux, Barossa, Tuscany, Napa, and other leading wine regions, because fine wine is now produced in many parts of the world, from Brazil to China. This accessible book also gives a flavor of other intriguing aspects, including the various key factors that contrive to make possible the vastly different styles of wines—dark and tannic, fresh and light, bone-dry, nectar-sweet, sparkling or sticky—how the industry recovered from some seriously crippling events during its long history, as well as some unfamiliar details of the business of wine.

Compiled by wine experts steeped in knowledge of their particular field of expertise, this book lets you master the art and craft of wine in 50 small sips—or a mere 300 words and one picture. Divided into seven sections, the topics cover the essential elements of wine beginning, naturally, with **The Vineyard**. Section two, **The Winery**, goes behind the label and explains how wine is made, from the pressing of grapes to the method for sealing the bottle. The most important grapes—the so-called international varieties—along with the finest expressions those grapes are capable of producing form the subject of section three. Then follow the highs and lows of wine's checkered history. Section five gives a bird's-eye

view of the top regions, from the centuries-old vineyards in Europe to those of the New World that now hold their own on the world stage, and the potential of emerging economies whose wines are attracting increasing attention. The final two sections, **the Business of Wine** and **Enjoying Wine**, offer a taste of the ways in which wine is sold and consumed. The beauty of this book is that you can choose to read it from beginning to end or simply select the topics that provide the most interest to you, with any technical or unfamiliar terms clearly defined in the glossaries. Finally, the people. The wine industry has produced a plethora of highly talented professionals, often entertaining characters. We have selected seven such personalities, all of whom have greatly influenced the course the wine industry has taken and had a major impact on making wine the magnificent beverage we can enjoy today.

This book might simply enable you to join the discussion the next time you and your friends are sharing a bottle of wine, or it might fuel a new passion for this sublime beverage. We hope you will enjoy this book as much as the contributors have enjoyed writing it.

Santé!
Gérard Basset OBE

THE VINEYARD

AOC (Appellation d'Origine Contrôlée)
See appellation

appellation A system of labeling quality wine to reflect a legally defined geographic area of production. It is intended to offer a guarantee of origin and quality, based on such factors as permitted grape varieties, style, and minimum alcoholic strength.

In France, where the modern-day appellation system was developed, **AOC** stands for *Appellation d'Origine Contrôlée*. At its heart is the notion of **terroir.** An AOC may be all-encompassing, such as "Bordeaux," or more specific, such as "Pauillac," which is a commune of Bordeaux. In Burgundy, AOCs even exist for individual Grand Cru vineyards, such as Le Montrachet.

Other countries have their own systems, although none as intricate as the French. The equivalent in Italy is **DOC** *Denominazione di Origine Controllata*), Spain uses **DO** (*Denominaciones de Origen*), and Portugal *Denominação de Origem Controlada* (**DOC**). The United States uses a system known as **AVA** (American Viticultural Area), while Australia has adopted **GI** (Geographical Indication).

Botrytis cinerea A benevolent fungus, also known as noble rot. It causes ripe grapes to shrivel and lose water content, thereby concentrating their sugars and other elements. Botrytized grapes are used to make sweet wines, such as Sauternes or Beerenauslese.

clone A copy of a grape vine traditionally propagated from a cutting of the original. It is more probable for clones today to be produced in a laboratory and grown for attributes, such as their yield or for resistance to disease, pests, frost, or drought.

IPM (Integrated Pest Management) An environmentally friendly approach to the control of pests, diseases, and weeds. While it eschews use of agrochemicals, it is not as stringent as organic viticulture, but brings economic, environmental, and safety benefits to the grape growers.

green harvesting The removal from the vine of a proportion of unripe bunches of grapes to concentrate the plant's energy on fewer grapes. Proponents claim the benefits include higher concentrations of sugars, tannins, and flavor in the remaining grapes. Skeptics note that many of Bordeaux's greatest vintages predate the green-harvest fashion and were naturally high yielding.

late harvesting Picking grapes long after they reach optimum ripeness to achieve even higher sugar levels. The risk is that the crop may be spoiled by adverse fall weather. Wines labeled

Late Harvest are usually sweet wines. The equivalent term in France is *Vendange tardive* and in Germany *Spätlese*.

lunar calendar In biodynamic viticulture, the lunar calendar is used to time critical aspects of vineyard management, including planting, weeding, harvesting, and the application of treatments, and even cellar management up to and including bottling. The vine's four components—root, leaf, flower, and fruit—are linked to the four elements of earth, water, air, and fire. Each component is said to be favored during particular points of the moon's cycle.

noble rot See *Botrytis cinerea*

Premier Cru, Grand Cru The quality classifications enshrined in the French Appellation (**AOC**) systems, but whose significance varies from region to region. *Cru* translates as "growth" and can refer to a single vineyard or group of vineyards. On Bordeaux's "Left Bank," only the five top wines are Premiers Crus Classés (First Growths). In St. Emilion, on the Right Bank, the top thirteen wines are known as Premiers Grands Crus Classés, with some 64 Grands Crus Classés estates ranked below them (see page 100). In Burgundy and Champagne, Grand Cru ("Great Growth") is the top-quality classification, followed by Premier Cru. Alsace has no Premier Cru classification, but almost 13 percent of its vineyards are classified Grands Crus.

rootstock The root of the vine onto which canes are grafted to produce fruit-bearing plants. Most rootstocks used today come from phylloxera-resistant, native American vine species or hybrids. *Vitis vinifera* is particularly susceptible to attack from the phylloxera louse. The most resistant American vine species are *V. riparia, V. rupestris,* and *V.berlandieri.*

varietal A wine made entirely (or almost entirely, depending on local wine laws) from a single grape variety.

vigneron/viticulturalist One who grows grapes and attends to all aspects of vineyard management. An oenologist studies or makes wine. Because grape quality is key in wine making, oenologists, especially consultants, are expected to have expertise in vineyard management.

vintage The grape harvest of a single year or the wine made from it.

Vitis vinifera The species of vine that is the source of most of the world's wine. There are many thousands of *vinifera* vines, all originally native to Europe and Central Asia.

TERROIR

3-SECOND SIP
Terroir encompasses the physical aspects of a vineyard—the location, altitude, aspect, soil—which, together with local climate, help define a wine from that vineyard.

3-MINUTE TOP OFF
Many explanations of terroir give the impression that a soil type is responsible for "flavoring" the wine; for example, grapes grown on limestone will somehow taste of limestone. This has not been proved; there is no link between soil type and wine style and quality. However, differences in soil type, soil depth, mineral composition, drainage, and water-holding capacity affect how the vine grows, which in turn affects crop level, how the grapes ripen, and thus the wine's style and quality.

The concept of terroir is one that underpins the Old World *appellation* system and is gradually finding favor in newer wine-growing regions. At its heart is location. Vines, although they may be of the same variety, clone, and rootstock, will grow differently in different locations, and the wine from those different locations will vary in character. Thus *terroir* is a shorthand way of explaining why all wines are unique. The vine is a sugar-producing plant and, subject to variety and wine style, the warmer the site, the better the wine—within limits, as conversely, too much sunshine and excessive heat can give low-acid, flabby-tasting wines. Therefore, well-sheltered vineyards, at favorable altitudes and facing south in the northern hemisphere or north in the southern hemisphere, produce riper grapes with better flavors and more substance and body than vineyards that are cooler and less well-situated. Add to this equation—which starts with the natural elements that are unchangeable—man-made factors, such as tradition, the variety and clone of the vine, planting density, pruning and training techniques, and, above all, the yield of the individual plot, and the reasons why one wine differs from another become clearer.

RELATED TOPICS
See also
THE VIGNERON
page 18

TRAINING & PRUNING
page 20

THE START OF APPELLATIONS
page 90

EXPERT
Stephen Skelton MW

It is now widely acknowledged that the nature and quality of a wine are—to a significant degree—defined by the place where the grapes are grown.

THE VIGNERON

3-SECOND SIP

Nurturing the growing grapes is the responsibility of the vigneron, whose every waking hour will be guided by the quality and yield level desired to produce a particular style of wine.

3-MINUTE TOP OFF

For the vigneron, there are certain times of the year when a single event can ruin the entire crop. Frost in spring, hail during summer, fungus on leaves and grapes during the growing season, a starling attack just as the bunches are ripening, can all spell disaster. Whether it is lighting heaters against the frost, warding off hail by sending rockets into hailclouds, spraying to prevent fungal diseases, or erecting netting against birds, a vigneron must be constantly vigilant.

Demand for better-quality wine has refocused attention on producing premium fruit; no other factor is more important. The vineyard cultivator, or vigneron, manages all aspects of growing grapes, taking into account local climate and soil conditions, and is responsible for every decision that affects fruit quality. This might include site selection, specifying the grape variety, clone and rootstock to be used, vineyard layout (whether up the slope or with the contours) and deciding on row width, distance between the vines, and the type of pruning and trellising systems to be used. The vigneron is also responsible for managing the annual tasks, from pruning in the dormant season, training the vines as they sprout their annual shoots, and nurturing the developing crop to ensuring that vines and fruit are not plagued by pests and diseases before the harvest. Additionally, tasks, such as deleafing the vines and crop reduction by thinning the bunches, might be required. The vigneron will also tend the vineyard soil, cultivating or mowing the land between the rows, and controlling weeds beneath the vines, even redistributing any of the precious soil washed down steep slopes by heavy rain.

RELATED TOPICS

See also
TERROIR
page 16

TRAINING & PRUNING
page 20

ORGANIC & BIODYNAMIC VITICULTURE
page 26

THE START OF APPELLATIONS
page 90

EXPERT

Stephen Skelton MW

The success of the annual grape harvest is a reflection of decisions made by the vigneron throughout the year as well as the vagaries of nature.

TRAINING & PRUNING

Vines are climbing plants and,

left to their own devices, would scramble over any available structure, seeking light and producing numerous tiny bunches of grapes. In order to produce the desired quantity and quality of fruit, commercial vineyards are arranged in rows for ease of access and harvesting, and growers have devised numerous ways of training vines onto trelliswork. Only rarely, in extremely dry regions (the island of Lanzarote, for instance), are vines grown unsupported along the ground. The aim is the same—ripe, healthy grapes —but training and pruning methods reflect climate, grape variety, wine style, regional traditions, and legal requirements of the appellation system. Pruning takes place a month or two after harvest, when the vines are dormant. Cooler climates favor high-density, cane-pruned vineyards; warmer regions tend toward lower-density, spur-pruned vineyards. Cutting back to a small amount of fruiting wood curtails vine vigor, limiting yield and ensuring that the grapes are as ripe as possible. During the growing season, the vines are trained up trelliswork so that the fruit receives maximum light and air, although in particularly hot climates some shading is encouraged to prevent the grapes from becoming raisins.

3-SECOND SIP
Vines must be managed—trained and pruned—to produce the right yield of grapes for the required wine: minute yields for ultra-premium wines; high yields for wines most people drink and enjoy.

3-MINUTE TOP OFF
Many factors determine how vines are trained, including the practicalities of working the land. On vertiginous inclines, as in Germany's Mosel, where tractor access is impossible, vines are trained onto single poles. Elsewhere, terraces are created on steep slopes to provide level surfaces for both vines and vehicles. On gentler gradients or flat land, higher-volume production is possible and vines appear in regimented rows, wide or narrow, depending on the equipment used.

RELATED TOPICS
See also
TERROIR
page 16

THE VIGNERON
page 18

3-SECOND BIOGRAPHY
JULES GUYOT
1807–72
French agronomist who devised the vine-management systems predominant in Bordeaux vineyards

EXPERT
Stephen Skelton MW

Variations on two pruning methods feature prominently in vineyards: cane pruning, where the fruiting wood is held on long canes; and spur pruning, where the annual fruiting wood comes from a cordon of older wood and is held on short canes (the spurs).

1922
Born in Vosne-Romanée, Burgundy

1939
With both his brothers on the front line, he leaves school to look after his family's vineyard holdings

1942
Marries Marcelle Rouget, a wine maker's daughter, who encourages Jayer into viticulture

1942
Commences oenology studies at the University of Dijon

1945
Signs a ten-year contract with the Noirot-Camuzet family to manage several of their Premier and Grand Cru plots and make the wines in return for 50 percent of the grapes

1945–50
Refines his wine-making techniques and sells his wines to négociants

1951
Leases vines in Richebourg, Vosne-Romanée, and Nuits-Saint-Georges; begins producing under his own label

1951
Buys, clears, and replants part of the Cros-Parantoux vineyard

1953
Successfully lobbies the INAO to promote Cros-Parantoux to Premier Cru status

1970
Purchases the final portion of Clos Parantoux from Robert Arnoux's sister

1978
Produces his first 100 percent Cros Parantoux wine, which becomes a sensational success in the United States

1995
Last official vintage of Clos Parantoux made by Jayer

1996
Retires and hands control to his nephew, Emmanuel Rouget, while continuing to make the wine, plus his own Réserve cuvée, until 2001

2001
Passes responsibility of his vineyards to Jean-Nicolas Méo and the running of the Domaine to nephew, Emmanuel Rouget

September 20, 2006
Dies in Dijon at the age of 84

2012
Jayer's private cellar sold at auction in Hong Kong; lot 98, just three bottles of Richebourg 1978, fetched HK$1,573,000 ($202,500)

HENRI JAYER

Henri Jayer gave the appearance of a modest Burgundian grower-winemaker, toiling in the vineyard and handcrafting wines in his modest cellar. Yet such was his following that when he died in 2006, every major newspaper from *Le Figaro* to *The New York Times* published his obituary. At auction in 2012, a case of his Vosne-Romanée "Cros Parantoux" 1985 sold for more than U.S. $250,000.

Jayer left school at sixteen years old to help his father tend the vines while his brothers went off to fight during World War II. In 1945, he signed a contract with the Noirot-Camuzet family to manage their Vosne-Romanée vineyards in return for a half share of the harvest. For the next few years, he made wine and sold it to négociants, all the time honing his skills.

Eventually; he inherited his father's 8.6 acres (3.5 hectares) of vines in Vosne-Romanée, Echézeaux, and Nuits-Saint-Georges and gradually augmented his holdings. His most significant purchase was part of the abandoned Cros Parantoux vineyard above the Grand Cru "Richebourg." Recognizing its potential, he cleared the scrub and boulders and replanted it with carefully selected Pinot Noir vines. It became one of Burgundy's most highly prized Premier Cru vineyards and was widely considered Grand Cru quality.

Jayer was well ahead of his time, believing in minimal intervention in both vineyard and cellar. He was one of the first in postwar Burgundy to oppose routine chemical spraying and to advocate plowing to control weeds. He also realized that low yields were the foundation of truly great wines long before that became the serious winemaker's mantra.

He believed adjustments in the cellar were unnecessary if the grapes were perfect, and so he often discarded up to 20 percent of his crop. He removed grape stems to avoid bitter tannins in his wines and was one of the pioneers of "cold soaking"—macerating grapes prior to fermentation to extract more flavor, aroma; and color. For reasons of hygiene, he fermented in concrete instead of wooden vats and, to avoid stripping wines of character, eschewed the widespread practice of filtration prior to bottling.

Considered normal today but groundbreaking at the time, Henri Jayer's techniques produced critically acclaimed wines said to be among the most richly textured, complex, and finely balanced ever made in Burgundy. Throughout his life, he maintained a reputation as one of the greatest vignerons of his era and inspired countless others to strive for perfection.

PHYLLOXERA

Phylloxera vastatrix is the Latin name of a destructive aphid, which in its root-louse form feeds on the roots of the European grapevine, *Vitis vinifera*, and over time so weakens them that they die. The aphid arrived in Europe from the east and southeast United States, where it is endemic and lives on wild vines—American vines—which have developed alongside the louse and are therefore tolerant of it. At the height of phylloxera's attack, nearly all of Europe's vineyards were affected. Despite desperate attempts to exterminate the pest, the only long-term solution was arrived at by grafting *vinifera* wood onto a rootstock developed from the louse-tolerant American vine, a practice now near-universal in Europe and elsewhere. Only in remote regions that have been isolated from the insect (Chile, for instance) are ungrafted vines grown on their natural roots. Grafting onto rootstocks brings other benefits, enabling vines to flourish in otherwise inhospitable conditions, such as limestone-rich, saline, or very dry soil, and in nematode-infested soil. However, growers in California who experimented with certain rootstocks tried varieties whose resistance to phylloxera was imperfect in their climatic and soil conditions and the bug was back, stronger than before, prompting a second epidemic at the end of the twentieth century.

3-SECOND SIP
In the nineteenth century, a small louse destroyed almost all of the world's vineyards, and it can still be a serious threat under certain circumstances.

3-MINUTE TOP OFF
Phylloxera (officially now called *Daktulosphaira vitifoliae*) is the deadly pest that brought the European wine industry to its knees in the second part of the nineteenth century, but it is by no means the vine's only enemy. Two forms of mildew, downy and powdery, are ubiquitous, while spiders, moths, mites, and bugs enjoy eating their way through grapevines, requiring vignerons to subject their vineyards to various remedies and treatments throughout the growing season.

RELATED TOPIC
See also
A CENTURY OF CRISES
page 88

3-SECOND BIOGRAPHY
JULES-ÉMILE PLANCHON
1823–88
French botanist who first identified phylloxera

EXPERT
Stephen Skelton MW

The scourge of the vineyard, phylloxera remains one of the biggest threats to the health of the grapevine.

ORGANIC & BIODYNAMIC VITICULTURE

Organic vineyards rely on naturally occurring materials—especially copper and sulphur—to protect vines against pests and diseases, and weeds are controlled by mulching and mechanical cultivation, instead of chemical herbicides. Synthetic fertilizers, fungicides, and pesticides are not permitted. Biodynamic viticulture takes organic viticulture to a level higher, akin to homeopathic medicine, and follows the teachings of Rudolf Steiner, who advocated a "whole-farm," self-sustainable approach to agriculture. It introduces the concept of self-healing by using certain preparations to stimulate the vine to produce its own defense mechanisms, including buried cow horn filled with manure or quartz, and composts that raise the numbers of worms and microorganisms in the soil to aid root development. Biodynamics also encompasses the use of a lunar calendar, which is held to promote planting success by dividing the days into four types—root, shoot, flower, and fruit—following the phases of the moon. Some highly rated vineyards have embraced organic and biodynamic principles and claim their wine quality has improved. Many growers follow a middle path, adopting Integrated Pest Management (IPM), which aims to reduce inputs by monitoring climatic conditions in order to predict diseases and the timing of pest attacks.

RELATED TOPIC
See also
THE VIGNERON
page 18

3-SECOND BIOGRAPHIES
RUDOLF STEINER
1861–1925
Austrian philosopher, scientist, and founder of the biodynamic movement

MARIA THUN
1922–2012
German biodynamic farmer and key figure in devising the sowing and planting calendar following the moon's phases

30-SECOND TEXT
Stephen Skelton MW

Belief that the moon affects life on Earth dates back to the observations of Pliny the Elder. Increasing numbers of growers are opting to work with, instead of against, nature.

THE WINERY

THE WINERY
GLOSSARY

barrel fermentation The process of alcoholic fermentation, usually at ambient cellar temperature, in small oak barrels. Wines fermented in new barrels (typically 60-gallon capacity) have a better integration of oak flavors than wines aged in new oak.

blend The mixing of selected barrels or smaller vats of wine to create a larger, homogenous quantity. It can also refer to wine made from several grape varieties. Most wines are blends. Médoc claret, for example, often comprises up to four varieties. Nonvintage Champagne blends wines from several vintages. The French term for blend is *assemblage* or *cuvée*.

carbonic maceration A way of making red wine starting with uncrushed bunches of grapes. Fermentation begins inside each berry until carbon dioxide, a by-product of fermentation, causes the grapes to burst, letting fermentation continue in the normal manner. The result is a more overtly fruity wine.

cooperage The activities and workplace of those who make and repair barrels and vats from staves of seasoned oak. Small barrels are often charred over a naked flame. The greater the charring, the more pronounced the aroma and flavor imparted to a wine.

Eiswein/Ice wine A sweet wine made from late harvested, naturally frozen grapes most commonly in Germany, Austria, and Canada. The frozen water content is removed after grape crushing, resulting in a wine of more concentrated sweetness, acidity, and flavor. Elsewhere, ice wine is occasionally made from artificially frozen grapes.

extract A word used to describe the body or weight of flavor of a wine. Technically, extract is the nonvolatile solids of a wine left after evaporation. They include sugar, acids, minerals, phenolics, trace elements, proteins, and pectins. Wines that are not filtered prior to bottling are higher in extract.

extraction The process of drawing phenolics (tannins and color) from grape solids into the wine during and after fermentation by various methods, such as pumping over and pressing.

lees The sediment or solids made up of spent yeast cells and other residue of fermentation. Generally, a newly made wine is left to settle and then racked (drawn) off its lees into a clean vessel. A wine may be given longer lees contact for added "yeasty" flavor, an example being Muscadet *sur lie* (on the lees).

maceration The steeping of grape skins and pulp in the grape juice or wine to extract color, flavor, and tannins. It can take place before, during, or after fermentation and may be manipulated by temperature or agitation of the liquid.

méthode champenoise (Champagne method) A term that uniquely describes the intricate process of making Champagne. Integral to the method is that the wine is grown, made, and bottled in the Champagne region of France. A landmark European legal case in 1994 ruled that no other region can use the term. Therefore, sparkling wines made in the same way elsewhere in France or Europe are commonly described as **méthode traditionelle** (traditional method).

must The sweet liquid that results from crushing of grapes prior to fermentation. It includes skins, seeds, pulp, and juice.

oenology The study of wine and wine making. Oenologists also have expertise in viticulture, because grape quality is integral to wine quality.

oxidized wine Wine that has lost its innate fruitiness due to overexposure to air. Since the Middle Ages, sulfur has been used in wine making to prevent oxidation. Controlled oxidation is part of the character of some classic wines, such as Oloroso sherry.

remuage The French word for **riddling**, part of the Champagne-making process. Bottles are periodically agitated by hand or by machines known as gyro-pallettes in order to gather **lees** from the second fermentation in the neck of the bottle ready for removal (disgorgement) before the bottle is topped off with fresh wine, corked, and secured with a wire cage.

tannin The drying, sometimes bitter or astringent element that forms part of the texture of red wine. It derives from the skins, seeds, and stems of grapes as well as from the oak in which a wine is aged. Pigmented tannins bind with other elements, such as potassium, calcium, and tartaric acid, over time to form sediment.

vat fermentation Alcoholic fermentation in large, inert vessels made of either wood, epoxy resin, glass-lined cement tanks, or stainless steel. The French *foudre*, a traditional wooden vat holding between 530 and 3,170 gallons, imparts no perceptible oak influence to the wine even when new—because of its relatively small surface area—compared to the volume of liquid it contains.

vinification The process of turning grapes into wine.

FERMENTATION

Louis Pasteur discovered the

microorganisms that play such an important role in all life's processes. Before his time, wine was made by leaving grape juice in an open vessel and waiting until the sweet grape juice was transformed into an intoxicating liquor that sometimes tasted pleasant. We now know that yeasts convert the sugars in grape juice into alcohol, simultaneously producing the flavors that indicate that this is wine. Alcoholic fermentations generally rely on the yeast *Saccharomyces elipsoideus* used by bakers and brewers. While this might be described as the common yeast, many indigenous yeast strains are present in the atmosphere that are not good at producing an attractive wine, so the majority of modern winemakers need to add a specially prepared culture. The range of different strains is huge, letting winemakers choose whichever gives the style required. There are yeasts that help to make the finest fizz, yeasts that produce enhanced aromas, yeasts that encourage high or low alcohols, and even special yeasts that produce the most delicate of fino sherries. They are all pampered creatures, preferring warm conditions and plenty of nutritious food. Unless yeasts get what they want, they sulk and die, leaving the winemaker with a major problem and a tankful of half-made wine.

Accident, trial and error, and advanced scientific knowledge have, over the centuries, enabled humans to enhance the metabolic power of yeast to produce a remarkable array of wines from a single source: fermented grapes.

SULFUR DIOXIDE

Sulphur dioxide is probably the winemaker's greatest ally, because it has many properties that help in the production of sound wine. But it is also the source of considerable controversy, because it is an unpleasant substance if misused. It has two particularly valuable properties, the best of which is that it is a powerful antioxidant and consumes oxygen quickly. Wine is a somewhat unstable liquid, being halfway between grape juice and vinegar. Yeasts convert the sugars in the grape juice to alcohol, but bacteria then convert the alcohol to acetic acid, which is the essential base of vinegar. However, this latter reaction depends on the presence of oxygen, which is abundant in the atmosphere and will dissolve in wine— oxidized wine rapidly loses flavor, color, and aroma. This is where sulfur dioxide plays its most important role as a preservative, attacking oxygen before it can damage the wine, thus maintaining the wine in a fresh and healthy condition. Its second property, curbing the activity of yeasts and bacteria, is no longer as important as it once was owing to the development of modern bottling techniques. A small but significant quantity of SO_2 is produced naturally during fermentation by the action of yeasts on the sulfur-containing compounds in the grape juice.

3-SECOND SIP
SO_2 is the most widely used of the small number of substances that winemakers are allowed to add to wine.

3-MINUTE TOP OFF
Sulfur dioxide is a widely used preservative in many foodstuffs, including sausages and dried fruits. Winemakers of the increasingly popular natural wine movement eschew the use of sulfur dioxide, regarding it as an unnecessary additive, but making good wine without it requires careful techniques to avoid dissolving oxygen from the atmosphere. European regulations require its presence to be indicated on the label, because it is an allergenic substance.

RELATED TOPICS
See also
CLOSURES
page 48

WINE & HEALTH
page 152

EXPERT
David Bird MW

A pungent, colorless gas seems an unlikely ingredient to find in food or beverages, but sulfur dioxide has been used to preserve quality and freshness in wine since ancient Roman times.

MAKING
WHITE WINE

RELATED TOPICS
See also
FERMENTATION
page 32

SWEET WINES
page 42

EXPERT
David Bird MW

3-SECOND SIP
White wines can be dry, sweet, or intensely luscious, and sweeter wines are often the best introduction to developing an enduring love of wine.

3-MINUTE TOP OFF
The world's great white wines tend to emanate from cooler climate regions, because white grapes require less warmth than black grapes to reach optimum maturity. Also, white wines need higher acidity than reds to maintain their refreshing nature, and acid levels fall with increasing temperature. Sweet whites need special techniques, including harnessing the ability of a benevolent fungus (*Botrytis cinerea*), the sun, or even ice to concentrate the juice to make gloriously intense dessert wines.

White wine is usually made

from white grapes, but it occasionally uses black grapes because most black grape juice is colorless. The simplest method is to harvest white grapes at optimum ripeness, and then crush and press them, collecting the juice for fermentation. The result will be white wine, but there are many refinements that can produce higher quality. Much of the grape's flavor lies in the skin cells, and unless these cells are broken the flavor is discarded with the skins. Fortunately, the cells containing the flavor compounds are fragile and easily rupture if the skins are macerated with the juice—this process is known as "skin contact." Making white wine from black grapes requires a different process because certain skin cells contain coloring substances, called anthocyanins, which, if the skins remain in the vat, turn the juice pink or even red. For example, when Pinot Noir is used to make still or sparkling white wine, the juice is separated from the skins immediately after the grapes have been pressed. Most—but not all— white wine is filtered for maximum clarity, although filtration can remove flavor as well as specks of solid matter.

White winemakers begin with the same simple process: grapes are pressed to release their juice and strained to remove the solids. The juice is pumped into a vat, yeast is added, and fermentation begins. Thereafter the options are varied, because white wines run the gamut of styles from bone dry to syrupy sweet, from sparkling to fortified.

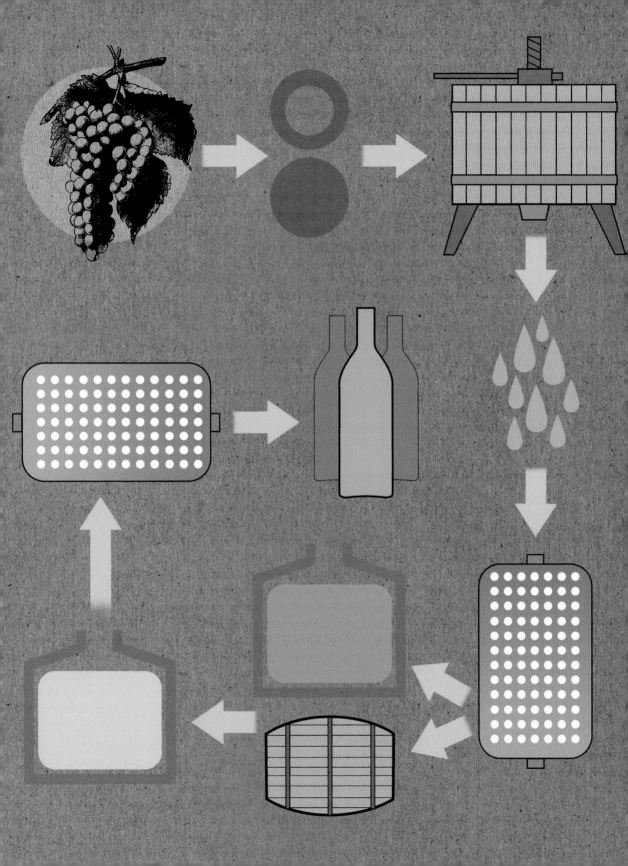

MAKING
RED WINE

3-SECOND SIP
Red wine styles range from light to dark and fruity to heavy or complex, and can be designed to be drunk almost as soon as they are bottled or built to last for decades.

3-MINUTE TOP OFF
In general, black grapes need more warmth than white grapes to reach full ripeness, which is why red wine production is more prevalent in the warmer parts of the world. Red wines, being vinified with the skins, develop powerful structure, flavor, and texture from the tannins in the skins. Tannins need time to soften and contribute to the wine's evolution, which explains why more red wines than whites are capable of improving over years— and tens of years.

Red wines are always made from black grapes. There is no alternative, because the red coloring material is found in the skin cells of these grapes, whereas the juice is usually colorless. Vinification also differs from that of white wine in that the skins are not separated from the juice after the grapes have been crushed, but are fermented with the juice so that the cells become soft enough to rupture and release the coloring matter and tannins. This is a critical part of the process, and the winemaker's expertise is of utmost importance. Time and temperature have a big effect on the wine's style: too long a maceration will yield a tough and bitter wine; too high a temperature will result in loss of fresh fruit flavors. The fermentation temperature is generally higher than in white wine making because of the need to extract the coloring matter from the skins, which is more efficient at higher temperatures. Fermentation normally continues until all of the sugars have been converted to alcohol, with the result that the vast majority of red wines are dry.

RELATED TOPICS
See also
FERMENTATION
page 32

AGING WINE
page 144

EXPERT
David Bird MW

The process for making red wine matches that for white, with one notable difference. The grape skins remain in contact with the wine during fermentation, which allows color and tannin to be drawn into the wine. Most reds are vinified dry or fortified; the amount of skin contact determines the style— rosé or light red to dark and tannic.

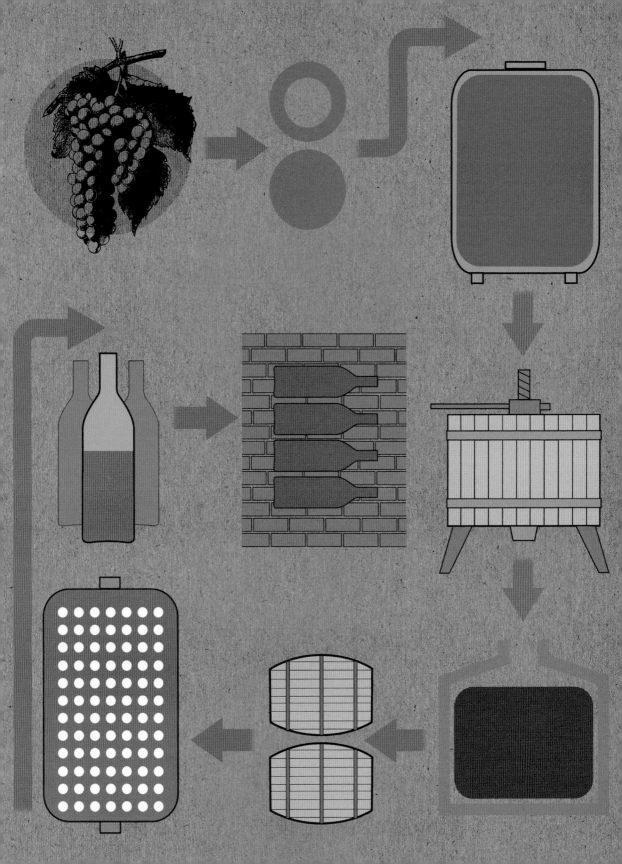

MAKING CHAMPAGNE

RELATED TOPICS
See also
FERMENTATION
page 32

WHY CHAMPAGNE SPARKLES
page 86

3-SECOND BIOGRAPHY
ANTOINE MÜLLER
1788–1859
German cellar master who,
with the widow Nicole-Barbe
Clicquot Ponsardin, devised
the technique of riddling

EXPERT
David Bird MW

3-SECOND SIP
The world-famous
sparkling wine produced
in the Champagne region
of France is made using
specified grape varieties—
Chardonnay, Pinot Noir,
and Pinot Meunier—and
according to highly
specified procedures, but
it is not the only wine
with bubbles.

3-MINUTE TOP OFF
This method is used around
the world, but it must be
referred to as *méthode
traditionelle*, because
Champagne makers are
protective of their product.
English sparkling wine uses
this method and is
particularly successful in
southern England, where
the grapes are grown on
Kimmeridge clay, the same
strata that appears in the
Champagne region.

The method known as *méthode champenoise* depends upon a fermentation in the bottle to produce the bubbles. The process starts with the production of a still, dry wine with all the grape sugars converted into alcohol. This wine is then bottled with the addition of a calculated quantity of sugar and some active yeasts. The bottles are then laid down in cold cellars hewn from the underlying chalk strata, where they mature for at least fifteen months (on the lees—the residual yeast) for Non-Vintage Champagne and thirty-six months for Vintage Champagne, during which time the yeasts feed on the sugar, converting it to alcohol, and producing the essential carbon dioxide that cannot escape. After maturation, the spent yeast has to be removed so that the finished wine remains clear when poured. Removal of this sediment is achieved by the complex process of remuage, or riddling, whereby small movements of the bottle gradually move the deposit into the neck of the bottle. By immersing the necks in a freezing bath, the deposit is trapped in a block of ice, which can then be expelled. The bottle is topped off with wine and a drop of sugar according to the style required, corked, labeled, and sold.

Unlike table wine, Champagne is bottled before fermentation is complete. It undergoes a second fermentation in the bottle and the process of riddling, in which the bottles are given a slight shake and turned, that helps loosen sediment thrown off by the second fermentation.

SWEET WINES

3-SECOND SIP

Sweet wines come in many styles, from delicate and elegantly sweet to rich and heavenly luscious.

3-MINUTE TOP OFF

Sweet wine's most important constituent, apart from sugar, are the natural acids that balance sweetness with a sharpness that refreshes the palate. Certain grape varieties possess this characteristic, such as Chenin Blanc in the Loire vineyards, and Furmint, used for the remarkable Tokaji Aszu wines of Hungary. The classic sweet wines of Sauternes are made with Semillon and Sauvignon Blanc, both recognized for their high acidity.

Wine is sweet when some of the grape sugar remains in the wine after fermentation has stopped naturally or been stopped by the winemaker. This residual sweetness is hard to achieve, because wine yeast will continue to feed on sugar until it cannot convert anymore into alcohol. Most sweet wines are produced only if the original grape juice ("must") contains more sugar than the yeast can consume. Sugar-rich fruit arises in several circumstances, the best being when grapes are attacked by a common mold, *Botrytis cinerea*, which develops under certain weather conditions. Instead of rotting, the grapes succumb to what is called "noble rot," slowly shriveling into raisinlike berries, producing wine of incredibly intense complex aromas and flavors, with an amazing sweet texture. Sauternes, from Bordeaux's legendary Château d'Yquem, or Germany's Trockenbeerenauslese produced by Egon Müller estate, are prime examples of these true marvels. Another way of concentrating the sugar is to let the grapes freeze on the vine during a hard winter frost to make Eiswein. The frozen grapes must be picked early morning and pressed quickly while still frozen, the ice crystals effectively removing some of the water from the juice. Elsewhere, in hot climates, harvested grapes are dried in the heat of the sun, which gives the same result.

RELATED TOPICS

See also
FERMENTATION
page 32

RIESLING &
SCHARZHOFBERGER
page 58

BORDEAUX
page 100

TUSCANY
page 104

EXPERT
David Bird MW

Judged by their appearance, late harvested grapes may seem to be well past their best, but their concentrated sugars can produce sublime dessert wines; letting the grapes freeze is one of many ways of doing this.

FORTIFIED WINES

Fortified wines—usually of

15–20 percent alcoholic strength by volume—can be made sweet, medium, or dry, depending on when spirit is added to the fermenting must (grape juice) or to the fully fermented wine. Sherry, from Jerez in southern Spain, is the most complex, because it ages under a veil of yeast, or *flor*, which changes the wine's characteristics while protecting it from oxygen. Most sherries are made from the Palomino grape—Moscatel and Pedro Ximenez are also used—and blended to a style ranging from sweet and viscous to delicate, bone-dry *fino*. In contrast, port—synonymous with its country of origin—is always sweet, because spirit is added much earlier in the fermentation, leaving residual sugar in the wine. Port styles are determined by the way the wine is stored. Ruby port resides briefly in large wooden vats before being transferred to tanks for blending. Tawny port undergoes maturation in small wooden barrels for ten, twenty, or forty years, depending on the style required. Vintage port is bottled after two years and then needs many more years in bottle. Other fortified wines include Madeira from the eponymous island (the best vintages of which are capable of being aged for decades), Marsala from Sicily, and Muscat from France (where it is called *vin doux naturel*), Australia, and California.

RELATED TOPICS
See also
FERMENTATION
page 32

AGING WINE
page 144

EXPERT
David Bird MW

Some of the world's most prized wines—sherry, Madeira, port, and Muscat—are fortified. The advantage of fortification is that it produces wines that are stable and can be kept for several weeks after opening.

ÉLEVAGE

3-SECOND SIP
Otherwise known as "raising up" or "maturation," élevage is the process, after fermentation that wine undergoes to bring it into the final state before bottling.

3-MINUTE TOP OFF
The final wine that goes into the bottle is a blend, even wine from great châteaux and famous domains. It will be a blend of wine made from grapes in different parts of the vineyard, perhaps from different varieties, using different vinification techniques—some from tanks to give freshness, some from barrels for complexity. The blender's skill is as important as that of the winemaker.

In modern wineries, most wines are fermented in stainless steel tanks, usually with automatic temperature controls. Sometimes the wine remains on the yeasty deposit (lees) in these tanks to develop extra complexity. But it isn't all high-tech; wooden and cement vats are returning to favor because their thick walls give good temperature stability, and one egg-shape, cement design produces natural convection currents without the use of mechanical stirring. During this period, there is an interplay between the spent yeasts and the wine's components that needs careful handling to avoid the production of unpleasant off-flavors. These reactions occur in anaerobic conditions—in the absence of oxygen—but this is not necessarily the optimum situation. Wine may be transferred to wooden containers to take advantage of the effects of gentle oxidation; the smaller the container, the greater the effect. The preferred wood is oak and its use has developed into a great art. Multiple decisions must be made regarding choice of oak and cooper (barrel-maker), whether to use large tanks or small barrels, how much toasting (charring) the barrel receives, its age (new oak flavors wine more than old), and how long the wine spends in the barrel. The winemaker's role is art and science in equal measure.

RELATED TOPICS
See also
HENRI JAYER
page 22

FERMENTATION
page 32

MICHEL ROLLAND
page 50

EXPERT
David Bird MW

The choice of vessel in which to ferment and age wine divides wine-making opinion, because the material used—oak (American or European), stainless steel, glass, or, increasingly, concrete—affects the flavor of the wine within.

CLOSURES

RELATED TOPICS
See also
ÉLEVAGE
page 46

HOW TO TASTE
page 146

EXPERT
David Bird MW

A high-quality natural cork is considered the ultimate closure, because it possesses the unique properties of sealing the bottle while allowing for easy withdrawal. It also lets the wine within mature perfectly, because the correct amount of oxygen can pass through the cork. The major problem with natural cork is the musty odor (termed "cork taint") that sometimes occurs in wine. The bark used to manufacture corks can harbor the microorganisms responsible for this aroma, but on occasions the musty odor can derive from sources other than the cork itself. Production of plastic stoppers that guarantee there can be no taint was tried briefly, but these stoppers proved ineffective at preventing oxygen entering the bottle. Thus the screw cap—a perfect oxygen barrier—became popular, but it acquired an image of being a cheap closure and is still not universally accepted by consumers. In addition, after it was discovered that its oxygen barrier was too efficient, manufacturers had to produce a screw cap that deliberately admits a controlled amount of oxygen into the bottle. In effect, the situation has come full circle. The message in the bottle is clear: there's more to closures than keeping the wine from flowing freely.

3-SECOND SIP
For millennia, cork has been the seal of quality for wine, but it can occasionally cause an unpleasant fault: corked wine.

3-MINUTE TOP OFF
The perfect closure is the holy grail for wine scientists concerned with cork taint and oxygen transmission rate (OTR). The new generation of winemakers can choose from a vast array of closures: natural cork of various grades; cork that has undergone manufacturing processes, including one that was invented for the production of decaffeinated coffee; plastic stoppers of various designs; glass stoppers; and screw caps. It's a competitive environment that ultimately benefits consumers.

A decent bottle of wine can be rendered undrinkable unless it is properly stoppered to ensure its carefully made contents are delivered as the winemaker intended.

December 24, 1947
Born in Libourne, France

1965
Enrolls at La Tour Blanche Viticultural and Oenology School, Bordeaux

1969–71
Attends Bordeaux's Institute of Oenology under Professor Emile Peynaud, "the forefather of modern oenology"

1973
Buys into the Chevrier Laboratory of Oenology in Libourne; subsequently becomes sole owner

1979
Takes over Château Le Bon Pasteur on the death of his father Serge

1986
Begins his international consultancy at California's Simi Winery, after an introduction from Robert Parker

1988
Takes on his first client in Argentina: the Etchart family of San Pedro de Yacochuya in Cafayate

1992
Creates the first white wine made on St. Emilion soil in modern times, at Château La Grande Clotte

1997
Laboratory moves from Libourne to larger premises in Catusseau, Pomerol

1998
Embarks on his personal project in Argentina, El Grupo de los Siete, with Bordeaux wine partners

2001
Establishes Campo Eliseo in Toro, Spain, with fellow luminaries Jacques and François Lurton

2004
Vilified in Palme d'Or-nominated documentary, *Mondovino*, which alleges his influence on the globalization of wine styles

2007
Starts The Rolland Collection, wines made from wholly owned estates and joint ventures

2013
Named the seventh most influential person in wine according to the *Decanter* Power List 2013

2013
Sells his family's Château Le Bon Pasteur to Chinese businessman Pan Sutong for an undisclosed sum

MICHEL ROLLAND

Bordeaux-based, globe-trotting

Michel Rolland is arguably the best-known and most influential oenologist in the world. He has been pivotal in steering many of his region's greatest red wines, and their international equivalents, toward a consistently riper, more opulent, and often oak-prevalent style.

Despite criticism from some quarters, he is in great demand, a consultant for more than 100 leading wine estates in 15 countries. Among them is the illustrious Château Ausone in St. Emilion; Pape Clément in Pessac-Léognan; Pontet-Canet in Pauillac; and one of Italy's Super Tuscans, Ornellaia. He works extensively in California for several highly regarded estates, including Harlan and Sloane Rutherford, as well as in Bulgaria, Greece, India, and Brazil. Currently, Rolland also owns or has an interest in ten geographically diverse wineries.

Rolland grew up at his family's Pomerol estate, Le Bon Pasteur, and, after graduating from Bordeaux's Institute of Oenology in 1971, he first joined; and then—together with his oenologist wife Dany—later bought the Chevrier Laboratory in Libourne. Mediocre vintages in the 1970s galvanized Rolland into promoting his belief that meticulous attention to vineyard health and cellar hygiene could transform wine quality, even in lesser years. While most oenologists remained in their laboratories, he routinely visited clients, persuading them to improve standards.

By the end of the 1980s, he was pioneering many of today's widely accepted practices. These include green harvesting, leaf plucking, and late picking to obtain optimum concentration and ripeness of the fruit. In the cellar, he enforced impeccable hygiene standards, promoted the benefits of new oak, and became renowned for his ability to blend harmonious and complex cuvées.

Some critics argue his wines have a certain "sameness," although the most prominent of all, Robert Parker, dismisses this as "absurd." While Rolland himself admits his preferred wine style is informed by his early love for wines such as Cheval Blanc 1947 and Latour '61, he is adamant that his objective "is not to produce First Growths everywhere, nor to make identical wines all around the world, but simply to allow each wine to express the full potential of its terroir."

CLASSIC GRAPES & WINES

1855 Classification A hierarchy of Bordeaux best wine estates drawn up for the Paris Exhibition of 1855. The rankings were based upon average market prices over many decades, and covered the red wines of the Médoc and the sweet wines of Sauternes-Barsac. The one geographical exception was the famous Château Haut-Brion, a Premier Cru Classé (First Growth) in the Graves region. The classification has remained intact for more than 150 years, although in 1973, Baron Philippe de Rothschild of Château Mouton Rothschild was successful in lobbying for his estate to be elevated to First Growth status under a decree signed by the then Minister of Agriculture Jacques Chirac.

aromatic wine A wine made from one or more grape varieties known for their pronounced aromatic qualities. These include Muscat, Riesling, Gewurztraminer, Sauvignon Blanc, and Viognier. Not to be confused with aromatized wine, which has been confected with herbs, spices, and other additives. (The Greek wine retsina has been aromatized with resin.)

backbone The term favored by wine professionals to describe the tannic structure (or "grip") of a red wine. The fruit is sometimes referred to as "flesh."

balance The overall harmony brought by the flavor and textural elements of a wine. To be considered well-balanced, a sweet wine, for example, requires balancing acidity; a tannic red, a certain amount of ripe fruit. If any one element stands out, such as excessive alcohol or searing acidity, a wine may be deemed unbalanced.

barrel fermentation The process of alcoholic fermentation, usually at ambient cellar temperature, in small oak barrels. Wines fermented in new barrels (with a typical capacity in the region of about 60 gallons) have a better integration of oak flavors than wines merely aged in new oak.

bodega A Spanish term for a winery, cellar, or wine firm.

Botrytis cinerea A benevolent fungus, also known as **noble rot** (*pourriture noble* in French). It causes ripe grapes to shrivel and lose water content, thereby concentrating their sugars and other elements. Botrytized grapes are used to make sweet wines, such as Sauternes or Beerenauslese. Botrytis develops naturally in certain vineyards in fall, subject to the right weather conditions. Outside of Europe, suitable vineyards are often deliberately inoculated with it for the production of dessert wines.

Côte-d'Or A French *département* and the heart of the Burgundy wine region, comprising the Côte de Beaune and the Côte de Nuits. Its capital is Beaune.

green The term used to describe the unpleasant characteristic of a wine made from underripe grapes. In a white, it may describe excessive tartness. In a red, it may relate to a lack of fruit and/or an imbalance of bitter tannins.

international varieties The grape varieties that stem from the classic wine regions of Europe and are today grown through the wine-producing world. The top varieties are sometimes termed the **noble grapes**. Among the reds these are Cabernet Sauvignon, Merlot, Pinot Noir, and Syrah/Shiraz. Among the whites, Riesling, Chardonnay, Semillon, Sauvignon Blanc, and Chenin Blanc.

lees The sediment or solids made up of spent yeast cells and other residue of fermentation. Generally, a newly made wine is left to settle and is then racked (drawn) off its lees into a clean vessel. A wine may be given longer lees contact for added "yeasty" flavor, an example being Muscadet *sur lie* (on the lees).

malolactic fermentation A secondary fermentation that occurs after alcoholic fermentation. Lactic bacteria converts a wine's harsh, malic acid into softer lactic acid with carbon dioxide as a by-product. It is encouraged in red wines and in some whites. In regions where wines suffer from a lack of fresh, natural acidity, malolactic fermentation is suppressed.

The Médoc The best-known wine district of Bordeaux that extends north of the city of Bordeaux, west of the Gironde estuary. It is often referred to as Bordeaux's "Left Bank" and most famously encompasses eight appellations, including the Haut-Médoc communes of Margaux, St. Julien, Pauillac, and St. Estèphe. It was the first Bordeaux region to be subject to an official hierarchy of estates, known as the **1855 Classification**, which is still in use today.

noble grapes See international varieties

CHARDONNAY &
LE MONTRACHET

3-SECOND SIP
Chardonnay produces some of the most elegant and beloved wines in the world, but suffers from its affable popularity.

3-MINUTE TOP OFF
Dubbed the "great white," the Chardonnay grape reaches its apogee in the form of a few thousand cases of wine produced from vines on a small strip of Burgundy named Le Montrachet. This famous slope has the ideal terroir: mineral-rich subsoil, perfect drainage, and a sheltered, southerly aspect for day-long exposure to the ripening rays of the sun. The result is one of the most complex—and costly—dry white wines made anywhere on Earth.

Chardonnay is the consummate politician. Comfortable in many guises, it readily changes its platform to suit its constituency and its flavors can range from citrusy green apples to buttery pineapple. Chardonnay's royalist home is Burgundy, where it is bottled under famed vineyard names, such as the revered Le Montrachet or, more populist, Meursault. The epitome of Chardonnay conservatism is Chablis in Burgundy's chillier north. Here, the wines are fresh, vigorous, and uncompromisingly austere. Chardonnay is also a key component in the world's finest sparkling wines, notably in the Champagne region, where famed bubblies, such as Dom Pérignon, rely on Chardonnay to achieve their elegance and finesse. Dubbed the "wine-maker's grape," Chardonnay's generous fruit readily responds to wine-making techniques such as barrel fermentation, lees contact, malolactic fermentation, or oak maturation. In the joyous revolutionary euphoria of the 1980s and 1990s, winemakers outside of the French appellations liberally employed all these techniques, each outvying the next with overt, dolled-up candidates. Like any healthy political system, there is plenty of opposition, and the reactionaries are now gaining momentum, especially in Western Australia, where unwooded Chardonnay has become a dark horse favorite.

RELATED TOPICS
See also
MAKING CHAMPAGNE
page 40

MEDIEVAL MONKS
page 82

THE JUDGMENT OF PARIS
page 92

BURGUNDY
page 102

EXPERT
Debra Meiburg MW

It is almost impossible to find a wine-making country that does not produce outstanding Chardonnay, the most ubiquitous of all the white grape varieties.

RIESLING & SCHARZHOFBERGER

3-SECOND SIP
In the pantheon of grape varieties, if Cabernet Sauvignon is the king, then Riesling is unquestionably the queen.

3-MINUTE TOP OFF
Egon Müller IV's wines command stratospheric prices. At auction in 2011, a mere 18 bottles of 1999 TBA achieved a record $4,900 (€5,300) per bottle. More modestly priced half bottles fetched a paltry $2,215 (€2,400). The wine has the viscosity of olive oil and a finish that lasts, literally, for minutes. Once tasted, it can never be forgotten. Riesling's many synonyms include Rhine Riesling, Johannisberg Riesling, and Weisser Riesling. Do not confuse with Welschriesling—which is neither true Riesling, nor a grape grown on the steep slate slopes of Mount Snowdon in Wales.

No grape matches Riesling for its ability to reflect the terroir in which it grows or the brilliant cut and clarity of its wines. It is one of the most aromatic white grapes. Peach, apricot, citrus, honey, herbs, and (sometimes) a surprisingly pleasant gasoline note, are identifiable, invariably balanced by exquisite acidity. Riesling is Germany's mainstay grape, and its most famous vineyard, the Scharzhofberger, in the Mosel region, produces some of the world's most sought-after wines. Ancestors of the current owner, Egon Müller IV, bought this vertiginous slate slope in 1797, and its wines have unparalleled poise. Elegant, yet paradoxically concentrated, with a wonderful mineral backbone, they improve for decades. Scharzhofberger Auslesen can be incredibly sweet and packed with ripe fruit flavors. Eiswein, made from frozen Riesling grapes, and botrytis-affected Beerenauslesen (BA) and Trockenbeerenauslesen (TBA) achieve the same miraculous qualities with such intensity and complexity that they have been known to make grown men weep. While Müller's Riesling is considered the *sine qua non*, a handful of other German estates, such as J. J. Prüm, produce equally fine examples. In neighboring Alsace, and Austria, Australia, and North America, the grape is frequently vinified dry.

RELATED TOPICS
See also
TERROIR
page 16

MAKING WHITE WINE
page 36

SWEET WINES
page 42

3-SECOND BIOGRAPHIES
NAPOLÉON BONAPARTE
1769–1821
French emperor who secularized many of Germany's finest vineyards

KATHARINA THANISCH
1865–1924
German widow who made the Mosel's first TBA in 1921

EXPERT
Martin Campion

Broadly speaking, German Riesling is graded by ripeness of the harvested grapes, ranging from Kabinett, the earliest picked, to Trockenbeerenauslese, a late-harvest, nectarlike dessert wine.

SAUVIGNON BLANC & POUILLY FUMÉ

3-SECOND SIP
Vibrant, zingy, and bracing, the adjectives describing Sauvignon Blanc are anything but bashful.

3-MINUTE TOP OFF
In the mid-1980s, New Zealand wineries, such as Cloudy Bay, produced a zinger of a wine that knocked the socks off the Loire Valley. However, maverick French winemaker Didier Dagueneau raised the bar by producing textbook examples of low-yield, barrel-fermented Sauvignon Blanc from the slaty soil of Sancerre and Pouilly Fumé. In terms of style, the world is again divided into two: those who love their Sauvignon barrel-fermented and those who prefer to leave its vibrant herbal fruit untamed.

The traditional home for this lively green-hued grape is northwest France, where the River Loire lazily snakes across a flat verdant landscape polka-dotted with sixteenth-century châteaux. The districts producing the Loire's finest Sauvignon Blanc are Sancerre and Pouilly Fumé, and these geographic designations are proudly displayed on labels. Sauvignon has long been served in Bordeaux, too, but until recently few producers took it seriously. In Pessac-Léognan, however, Sauvignon Blanc grapes are fermented and matured in oak barrels and rank among the world's most revered. While Sancerre and Pouilly Fumé have long held sway with Europeans, it was New Zealand that put the variety on the global map. When pouring New Zealand Sauvignon Blanc, expect exuberant guava, passion fruit, kiwi, and gooseberry flavors with herbal, grassy accents and brisk acidity. Other countries also welcomed this irascible sometimes grassy grape (Sauvignon derives from the French word *sauvage*, meaning "wild"). South Africa made a name for its Sauvignon by largely eschewing the green edges found in versions from New Zealand and Chile. Basking in the sunny Cape, the grapes produce a full-figured wine with tropical fruit nuances and high alcohol levels matched only in California.

RELATED TOPICS
See also
BORDEAUX
page 100

MARLBOROUGH
page 112

3-SECOND BIOGRAPHY
DIDIER DAGUENEAU
1956–2008
French winemaker who produced exemplary Sauvignon Blanc in the Loire Valley

EXPERT
Debra Meiburg MW

The early-ripening, aromatic Sauvigon is the white grape of the upper Loire region of France and the variety that has become synonymous with New Zealand's output.

CABERNET SAUVIGNON & CHÂTEAU LATOUR

3-SECOND SIP
Renowned for its elegance and longevity, on its own Cabernet Sauvignon can be a demanding, tannic wine, so Merlot and Cabernet Franc usually step in to smooth its tough edges, rounding it out with gentle plummy fruit.

3-MINUTE TOP OFF
Cabernet Sauvignon is avidly collected by wine connoisseurs and reaches its apogee in Bordeaux, where it produces the longest-lived wines in the world. In a ranking of Bordeaux's wines in 1855, Château Latour was generally considered the finest wine of Bordeaux's Médoc area. It still is. Stern and austere in youth, this classic emblem of Bordeaux is fiercely treasured by wine lovers.

It's not easy being a king.

Cabernet Sauvignon bears the weighty crown of global adulation, but like any successful monarch, this thick-skinned variety has the loyal support of other influential members of the nobility: Merlot and Cabernet Franc. Dark-colored Cabernet Sauvignon ranges from medium to full-bodied, delivering sumptuous red and black-currant flavors accented with warm spice, tobacco, graphite, and leather. Most wine regions warm enough to ripen it will grow at least a small amount of Cabernet Sauvignon, but its seat of power has always been Bordeaux's Left Bank, where this regal grape produces dense wines with crisp acidity and compact, linear tannins. In cool climates, this variety battles for ripeness and can have green, weedy aromas and intensely astringent tannins, but from warm realms—Australia, California, Chile, and South Africa—plush blackberry, mulberry, and plum leap from the glass. Cabernet Sauvignon is also one of the world's most popular blending partners, used to give backbone to varieties such as Sangiovese, Shiraz, or Tempranillo. Cabernet reigns supreme at the dinner table, where its tannins make dynastic alliances with fatty dark meats, such as roast duck, grilled steak, or rack of lamb.

RELATED TOPICS
See also
BORDEAUX'S RISE TO PROMINENCE
page 84

THE START OF APPELLATIONS
page 90

BORDEAUX
page 100

WINE INVESTMENT
page 136

3-SECOND BIOGRAPHY
FRANCOIS PINAULT
1936–
French business and art collector and the current owner of Château Latour

EXPERT
Debra Meiburg MW

Bordeaux's most famous red grape, Cabernet Sauvignon is equally at home around the globe from Barossa to Beijing, Chile to Canada.

PINOT NOIR & LA ROMANÉE-CONTI

RELATED TOPICS

See also
MEDIEVAL MONKS
page 82

THE START OF APPELLATIONS
page 90

BURGUNDY
page 102

PRODUCERS
page 126

3-SECOND SIP

Soft red fruit, silky texture, and perfumed with delicate nuances of violets, fall leaves, or leather, nothing's sexier than Pinot Noir.

3-MINUTE TOP OFF

Pinot Noir producers are an impassioned bunch and crop up the world over, seeking this holy grail of wines. Cool-climate sanctuaries in New Zealand, the United States, and Australia produce sublime examples, but the most hallowed Pinot Noir comes from a few hectares in the heart of Burgundy, owned by Domaine de la Romanée-Conti (DRC). Its most precious vineyard, La Romanée-Conti, grows the grapes that make the most exquisitely scented and textured of all Pinot. It is also possibly the most expensive red wine on the planet.

Pinot Noir is as sheer as a negligée and almost always pale ruby in color when made into red wine. If you can see your date through the wine glass, surely you are sipping a Pinot. In wine terms, light color is synonymous with light body, and it is lightness that makes Pinot Noir such a versatile food match. Delicately perfumed with aromas of strawberries, red cherries, and raspberries, Pinot Noir is matured in oak but always to add the merest elusive touch so that the wood never overwhelms the fruit. The temperamental princess of black grapes, Pinot Noir's color, aroma, and texture are greatly affected by vineyard climates and soil, so Pinot varies considerably from place to place. The ancient wine-growing district of Burgundy is Pinot's royal seat, its cool springs and warm summers providing perfect conditions for fussy Pinot Noir. While the grape has reigned supreme in Burgundy's Côte d'Or for centuries, it is also the backbone of France's famed Champagne district. Here, Pinot Noir's black grapes are harvested and crushed with the juice immediately run off the skins to ensure the wine remains clear-colored—hence white wine from black grapes: Blanc de Noirs.

3-SECOND BIOGRAPHY

AUBERT DE VILLAINE
1940–
French coowner and codirector of Domaine de la Romanée-Conti

EXPERT

Debra Meiburg MW

Thin-skinned and fickle, Pinot Noir is the grape that seduces red wine producers the world over, bewitched by the peerless quality of truly great red burgundy.

SYRAH/SHIRAZ & HERMITAGE

3-SECOND SIP

Not many varieties can wear two hats—let alone two names—but the mighty Syrah is not just any variety.

3-MINUTE TOP OFF

Oddly, top producers often chuck handfuls of white Viognier clusters into the fermentation tanks with inky, dark-purple Syrah. They insist Viognier softens Syrah and increases complexity. However, the maker of Australia's most iconic wine, Penfolds Grange, relies on Cabernet Sauvignon to give Shiraz added dimension. Widely considered Australia's most collectible wine, Penfolds Grange—dubbed Australia's "first growth" wine—sources fruit from a range of South Australian vineyard sites and lasts for decades.

France's northern Rhône Valley originally set the benchmark for fine-quality Syrah, a black grape the Australians adopted and, in a smart marketing move, dubbed "Shiraz" a century ago. Their wines are distinctively different from classic Rhône style. Shiraz from Australia is a fruity, friendly, tail-wagging puppy of a wine; the same grape grown in France produces a more restrained, almost saintly, drop. The north Rhône is Syrah's spiritual home and the 300-acre Hermitage its finest appellation; the wines seemingly live forever and tend to be lean and firm, with aromas reminiscent of smoked meats, leather, red berries, and earthy black truffles. Shiraz is the Australian flagship variety, its wines rich and spicy, with violet and wild black fruit aromas. Gutsy, meaty wines from the warm Barossa Valley, Eden Valley, McLaren Vale, and Clare Valley set the standard. In cooler Australian sites, the grapes assume a gentle red fruit lightness, evoking savory dried herbs with peppery accents. The love affair with this deep-purple variety echoes in other wine-producing countries such as Chile, Argentina, South Africa, New Zealand, and the United States, assuming either name. Increasingly, most label their wines Syrah, but occasionally a winemaker producing clean, fruit-forward, plush wine will don an Akubra hat and call it Shiraz.

RELATED TOPICS

See also
REGIONAL GRAPE
& WINE STYLES
page 74

BAROSSA VALLEY
page 114

WINE INVESTMENT
page 136

3-SECOND BIOGRAPHY

MAX SCHUBERT
1915–94
Australian winemaker who created Penfold's Grange Hermitage

EXPERT

Debra Meiburg MW

Syrah or Shiraz, depending on the latitude, is one and the same—the grape that makes some of the most dark-hued, full-bodied red wines in the world.

January 1948
Born in Wales, UK

1953
Emigrates to Canada
with parents

1959
Moves to California
with parents

1977
Gains a PhD in Genetics
from University of
California, Davis

1977–78
Postdoctoral Fellow,
Department of Crop and
Soil Sciences, Michigan
State University

1978–80
Research Biologist,
Stauffer Chemical Co.,
Richmond, California

1980
Works as assistant
professor and researcher
at the Department of
Viticulture and Enology
at the University of
California, Davis

1986
Purchases property on
Mount Veeder in Napa
and moves there with
husband Stephen Lagier,
while continuing to
commute to UC Davis

1990
Named Fellow, American
Association for the
Advancement of Science

1994
Plants first vines at
Lagier Meredith
Vineyard, Napa

1998
The Lagier Meredith
Vineyard produces its
first commercial wine

2000
Awarded the title of
Chevalière de l'Ordre du
Mérite Agricole by the
French government

2003
Retires from UC Davis

2009
Inducted into the
California Vintners Hall of
Fame in Napa Valley

CAROLE P. MEREDITH

Carole Meredith is an American grape geneticist and professor emerita in the Department of Viticulture and Enology at the University of California, Davis. During her research career, she pursued several aspects of grapevine genetics, including genetic engineering and genome mapping. She is credited with discovering the history and place of origin of several significant grape varieties, including Cabernet Sauvignon, Chardonnay, Syrah, and Zinfandel—subjects of speculation for more than a century.

Traditionally, the identification and classification of grapevines belonged to the field of botany known as ampelography. It involves comparing the shape and color of vine leaves, grape berries, and their constituents. Since the 1990s, the study of vines has been revolutionized by DNA typing (or "fingerprinting"), a field in which Meredith and her research team became world leaders. By extracting and manipulating the DNA from the leaves and shoots of vines, she was able to establish patterns unique to individual varieties.

Soon after this initial breakthrough, Meredith formed a multinational genetics cooperative (International Vitis Microsatellite Consortium), through which researchers everywhere could pool their findings on so-called DNA markers in grapevines. This led to an explosion of knowledge in grape varieties, their origins, and interrelatedness.

One of Meredith's early pronouncements was to confirm that California's Zinfandel and southern Italy's Primitivo were one and the same variety. In 2000, working with researchers from the University of Zagreb, she established this vine was also identical to a near-extinct Croatian variety, Crljenak Kaštelanski.

In 1997, with colleague Professor J. E. Bowers, Meredith revealed Cabernet Sauvignon to be a crossing of Cabernet Franc and Sauvignon Blanc. This discovery was followed by the revelation that Pinot Noir had parented no fewer than sixteen well-known grape varieties. Its offspring include Chardonnay, the Gamay grape of Beaujolais, and Muscadet's Melon de Bourgogne. Publication of these findings in 1999, in the prestigious journal *Science*, reflects their importance to the scientific community at large.

As well as being historically intriguing to serious wine lovers everywhere, Meredith's pioneering research has practical implications for the conservation of grape varieties and for avoiding genetic inbreeding among vines. It has broadened the horizons for grapevine breeders aiming to develop new varieties resistant to pests, diseases, and even adverse climatic conditions.

Meredith retired from academia in 2003 to devote more time to her wine estate, which she owns with her husband Stephen Lagier in the Mount Veeder district of Napa Valley.

TEMPRANILLO & RIBERA DEL DUERO

3-SECOND SIP
An easy-drinking wine compatible with a range of foods, Tempranillo may be the gem of Spanish viticulture, but it is one of Australia's fastest-emerging varieties.

3-MINUTE TOP OFF
Tempranillo assumes more aliases than a CIA agent. The grape has about fifteen pseudonyms in Spain alone, ranging from the straightforward Tinto Fino in Ribera del Duero to the tongue-twisting Ull de Llebre ("eye of the hare") in Catalonia. In port wines, Tempranillo assumes the name Tinta Roriz. Perhaps Tempranillo has such a long list of aliases because it is not an easy grape to pin down. Descriptions such as strawberry, plum, and tobacco leaf are helpful but limited.

Tempranillo is such an early ripening grape that its name was coined from the Spanish word for "early": *temprano*. Its wine sings with red fruit and has silky tannins, similar to Pinot Noir, but with soft, gentle acidity. Inseparable from Spain, Tempranillo is so ubiquitous in the Spanish landscape that one is hard-pressed to find a region without this affable vine. Across the grape's northern stronghold, Rioja and Ribera del Duero stand out; both regions produce long-lived, high-quality Tempranillo. In Rioja, the source of Spain's best-known red wine, Tempranillo is dominant, usually topped off with two other varieties, Grenache and Carignan, and tends to be lighter-bodied than wines from Ribera del Duero, which are more dense, tannic, and powerful. Ribera's—and Spain's—most revered wine is Vega Sicilia's Unico, a stunning Tempranillo backed by Cabernet Sauvignon. A thirsty public must also be patient. The lush, elegant, spicy wine from this 150-year-old bodega is aged for at least a decade in barrel and bottled before its release. Spain's penchant for maturing Tempranillo in American oak integrates vanilla and coconut aromas into the wine, bringing to mind a strawberry and vanilla ice cream. With age comes reverence: Tempranillo develops a complex leather and autumnal bouquet.

RELATED TOPICS
See also
REGIONAL GRAPES
& WINE STYLES
page 74

RIOJA
page 108

WINE INVESTMENT
page 136

3-SECOND BIOGRAPHY
PABLO ÁLVAREZ
fl. 1982–
Unassuming CEO of Vegas Sicilia and producer of Unico, a Tempranillo blend widely revered as Spain's finest wine.

EXPERT
Debra Meiburg MW

Vibrant, savory Tempranillo, once a local hero of northern Spain, has now become a major player on the international wine scene.

NEBBIOLO & BAROLO

RELATED TOPIC
See also
TUSCANY
page 104

3-SECOND SIP
Nebbiolo tantalizes with an exotic array of cherry and damson fruit, aniseed, dried herbs, or licorice spices, and an earthiness reminiscent of truffles, leather, and tar.

3-MINUTE TOP OFF
This ancient variety was so greatly prized in Piemonte that a series of penalties was devised to deter ambitious neighbors from pilfering cuttings. In the fifteenth century, the statutes of La Morra village ordered a five-lire fine levied on sneaks who pirated Nebbiolo vine cuttings. A few pages later, the statutes prescribed lopping off the hands of repeat offenders, with hanging recommended for unapologetic looters who damaged more than 15 vines.

Three years before Kublai Khan founded the Yuan dynasty, writers were praising the Nebbiolo grape of northern Italy's Piemonte region. Described as *nibiol* in 1268, its name is based on the Latin root *nebula*, meaning "fog" or "mist." Most authorities believe it is known as the "fog grape," because it ripens significantly later than other red varieties—not until late September and October, when autumnal mists shroud Piemonte's hills and the white truffle season begins. Light-hued Nebbiolo is often compared to Pinot Noir because both are notoriously finicky, site-sensitive varieties. But when the gods align, their haunting aromas and ethereal elegance are unmatched in the wine world. Unlike Pinot Noir, Nebbiolo has had limited success outside its ancestral home. Winemakers in California, Australia, Chile, and Argentina have fussed and fiddled with the grape, but it never reaches the glorious complexity and regal bearing of Piemonte's top sites, Barolo and Barbaresco. Youthful Nebbiolo is obdurately tannic and acidic, but after a decade or more its tannins have matured to a soft dustiness. Unquestionably, Giacomo Conterno reigns supreme as Piemonte's winemaker producing iconic Barolo, an exquisite wine derived fromthe cluster of villages oft-cited as producing "the wine of kings and the king of wines."

Quintessentially Italian, Nebbiolo is rarely seen beyond Piemonte where, in the right hands, it produces some of the slowest-maturing of all red wines with the haunting aromas of its hilltop home.

REGIONAL GRAPES & WINE STYLES

3-SECOND SIP

Grape variety, geographical location, and alcohol levels largely determine style, but all wines can be loosely divided into light-, medium-, or full-bodied.

3-MINUTE TOP OFF

Fat, round, or lean, we're all obsessed with body image. Just like humans, wine comes in different weights or styles, but it is important that the weight is in balance with its fruity character, acidity, sweetness, and alcohol content. Without sufficient flavor to round out the delicacy, however, the wine is disparagingly described as thin.

Beyond the familiar "international" grapes are regional varieties, historically rooted to a place and adapted to its terroir. Appellation laws specified which grapes could be planted to preserve a wine's identity—so Hungary's Tokaji must be made with the Furmint grape and Stellenbosch red Cape Blends always include the distinctively South African Pinotage. Variety primarily determines a wine's weight or style, but location is important. Warm climates produce high-alcohol wines, and typically reds from such climes are full-bodied, heavy, dark-hued with concentrated fruit; consider Malbec (Argentina), Zinfandel (California), Aglianico (Italy), Carmenere (Chile), Mourvedre, and Tannat (southern France). Cool climates normally yield lightly pigmented grapes, hence lighter-bodied, delicate wines, such as Italy's Bardolino from Corvina and Rondinella grapes grown beneath the alpine foothills. Light white wines, pale as water, are easily spotted and include Pinot Grigio (Italy), Chenin Blanc (France, South Africa), Albarino, Verdehlo (Spain), and Torrontes (Argentina). Medium-weight whites encompass delicate and floral Arneis (Italy), Assyrtiko (Greece), and savory Grüner Veltliner (Austria). Apricot-scented Viognier (France, New Zealand, United States) is a full-bodied white grape, but the white heavyweight champion is an aromatic globe-trotter: Gewurztraminer.

RELATED TOPICS

See also
TERROIR
page 16

THE START OF APPELLATIONS
page 90

HOW TO TASTE
page 146

FOOD & WINE
page 148

EXPERT
Debra Meiburg MW

From Assyrtiko to Zinfandel, the array of hundreds of grape varieties is at once exciting and daunting, although all wines can be more readily identified by their style.

HISTORY

1855 Classification A hierarchy of Bordeaux best wine estates drawn up for the Paris Exhibition of 1855. The rankings were based upon average market prices over many decades, and therefore covered the red wines of the Médoc and the sweet wines of Sauternes-Barsac. The one geographical exception was the famous Château Haut-Brion, a Premier Cru Classé (First Growth) in the Graves region. The classification has remained intact for more than 150 years, although in 1973, Baron Philippe de Rothschild of Château Mouton Rothschild was successful in lobbying for his estate to be elevated to First Growth status under a decree signed by the then Minister of Agriculture Jacques Chirac.

blind tasting An objective form of wine tasting in which participants assess the quality of a wine, and in some instances try to determine its precise origin, without knowing its identity. Its prime benefit is to eliminate the prejudices inferred by price, name, and region.

claret A uniquely Anglo-Saxon term, originating from the Middle Ages, for the red wines of Bordeaux. At the time, red and white grapes were grown alongside each other in the vineyard and vinified together, producing a lighter-colored red than is the norm today. The French called it *clairet*, meaning "light red."

disgorgement The part of the traditional sparkling wine-making process that expels sediment (the residue of a second fermentation) from the neck of the bottle. Invented by the Veuve (Widow) Clicquot in 1816, manual disgorgement inevitably wasted a quantity of Champagne. The long foil on the neck of a bottle was to hide the fact that it was not full. Modern disgorgement involves freezing the neck in order to expel only the frozen sediment prior to the bottle being topped off.

méthode champenoise (Champagne method) A term that uniquely describes the intricate process of making Champagne. Integral to the Champagne method is that the wine is grown, made, and bottled in the Champagne region of France. A landmark European legal case in 1994 ruled that no other region can use the term. Therefore, sparkling wines made in the same way elsewhere in France or Europe are commonly described as **méthode traditionelle** (traditional method).

remuage The French word for riddling, which is part of the Champagne-making process. Racked bottles are periodically agitated by hand or by machines known as gyro-pallettes to gather lees from the second fermentation in the neck of the sealed bottle ready for **disgorgement**.

Premier Cru, Grand Cru The quality classifications enshrined in the French Appellation (**AOC**) systems, but whose significance varies from region to region. *Cru* translates as "growth" and can refer to a single vineyard or group of vineyards. On Bordeaux's "Left Bank," only the five top wines are Premiers Crus Classés (First Growths). In St.Emilion, on the Right Bank, the top thirteen wines are known as Premiers Grands Crus Classés, and some sixty-four Grands Crus Classés estates ranked below them (see page 100). In Burgundy and Champagne, Grand Cru ("Great Growth") is the top-quality classification, followed by Premier Cru. Alsace has no Premier Cru classification, but around 13 percent of its vineyards are classified Grands Crus.

rootstock The root of the vine onto which canes are grafted to produce fruit-bearing plants. Most rootstocks used today come from phylloxera-resistant, native American vine species or hybrids. *Vitis vinifera* is particularly susceptible to attack from the phylloxera louse. The most resistant American vine species are *Vitis riparia, V. rupestris,* and *V. berlandieri*.

varietal A wine made entirely (or almost entirely, depending on local wine laws) from a single grape variety. The concept was pioneered in California as early as the 1950s and 1960s, but really gained traction in the 1970s, when Napa Valley winemakers, such as Robert Mondavi, began marketing Cabernet Sauvignon and Chardonnay. Varietal wines soon became the norm in other New World countries, especially Australia, New Zealand, and South Africa. A varietal wine is distinct from one named after its region of origin (or inspiration), such as Chablis, Burgundy, and Champagne.

WINE'S SPIRITUAL BEGINNINGS

3-SECOND SIP

Wine began as a spiritual, not a secular, good, and for much of its history was consumed as a way of communing with the divine.

3-MINUTE TOP OFF

The ancients may have regarded wine as heavenly alchemy, but by all accounts it did not taste heavenly. When exposed to too much air, all wine turns sour. To disguise its vinegariness, winemakers added myriad flavorings— herbs, spices, honey, marble dust, myrrh, and, most notably, pine resin. The most valued wines were invariably those with the most flavorings. Thick and oily, they tasted more syrupy than sublime.

For most of its eight thousand-year history, wine was not prized primarily as a source of pleasure or even sustenance but, instead, as a means of communion with one's god or gods. Fermentation, being a natural process, meant that the transformation of fresh grape juice into alcoholic wine could occur without human hand, making the beverage seem magical, mysterious—surely divine intervention? And because wine made people feel good, it seemed to promise connection to a supernatural or transcendent realm. In ancient cultures, from Neolithic Transcaucasia (where wine was first drunk regularly) to Anatolia, the Levant, Egypt, Greece, and Rome, wine was deemed to be a gift from the gods. It was at heart spiritual, and imbibing offered a way to literally sense the divine nature of creation. Especially in classical Greece and then in Rome, where drinking became commonplace, the heady beverage also provided indulgence—sometimes debauched— for the rich and nourishment for the poor. But until the rise of a religion that distinguished sharply between secular and sacred, wine never lost its spiritual essence. For early Christians, communion wine—the Blood of God—was very different from the drink that slaked thirst or quickened passion. In previous cultures, however, all wine was equal: heavenly because godlike.

RELATED TOPICS

See also
FERMENTATION
page 32

MEDIEVAL MONKS
page 82

3-SECOND BIOGRAPHIES

DIONYSUS
Greek wine god who lived on in ancient Rome under the name Bacchus

EURIPIDES
ca. 480–406 BCE
Greek tragedian whose *Bacchae* depicts Dionysus as inhabiting the wine itself

PLINY THE ELDER
23–79 CE
Roman author whose *Natural History* provides a detailed record of early wine culture

EXPERT

Paul Lukacs

Wine has been revered, blessed, and enjoyed throughout the ages by rulers, popes, and ordinary people.

MEDIEVAL MONKS

RELATED TOPICS
See also
TERROIR
page 16

BURGUNDY
page 102

A small fraternity of white-habited monks made the most celebrated wines in Europe during the Middle Ages. They discovered what centuries later came to be called terroir, the magical ability of a particular place to impart an identifiable character to the wines made from grapes grown there. These monks belonged to the Cistercian order, an exceptionally devout society that shunned worldly wealth but embraced manual labor. Starting in Burgundy, they recorded in meticulous detail which vineyard plots produced the healthiest crops. Only a few paces could separate an excellent site from an ordinary one, and the monks constructed stone walls around the best, designating each one as a *clos*—a cloistered, enclosed place. The wines from those places tasted special because different—and different because particular. They became the favorites of kings and queens, dukes and bishops—and even popes. Before long, lay farmers adopted similar practices in their own vineyards, and the new focus on place expanded to include parts of Alsace, the Loire and Rhône valleys, and the hillsides along both the Mosel and Rhine rivers in Germany. By literally rooting the character of their wines in the singularity of place, the Cistercian monks had given wine something it never had before—individuality.

3-SECOND BIOGRAPHIES
BERNARD DE CLARVAUX
1090–1153
French abbot and the founder of the Cistercian order

POPE URBAN V
1310–70
Provençal Benedictine who refused to move to Rome in part because he loved the new Burgundy wines

EXPERT
Paul Lukacs

Monks assumed the habit of wine making established by the ancients, developing vital techniques and identifying many of the finest vineyards in Europe.

BORDEAUX'S RISE TO PROMINENCE

3-SECOND SIP
A style of red Bordeaux, tasting unlike any made before, emerged in the mid-seventeenth century, and by 1800, it had become the most prestigious wine in the entire world.

3-MINUTE TOP OFF
During the first half of the nineteenth century, various people tried to organize or rank the wide range of red Bordeaux wines coming onto the market every year. In 1855, an official committee issued a report in which they classified the region's top wines, the first growths being those that consistently fetched the highest prices. That report, known as the Bordeaux 1855 classifcation, still holds sway today.

"A good and most particular taste" is how the English diarist Samuel Pepys described his first experience with the new red wines coming from Bordeaux in the seventeenth and eighteenth centuries. Wine had been made in the marshy lowlands between the Garonne and Dordogne rivers since the Romans first occupied the region. During the Middle Ages, *clairet*, a pinkish blend, became popular in northern Europe, where trade in it made many fortunes. Like most medieval wines, however, it tasted generic instead of particular, and so was a far cry from the dark red that Pepys admired. The new breed of red Bordeaux, led by those from an estate called Haut-Brion, displayed distinctive flavors and aromas. Sometimes called "clarets," they tasted special because they were particular. Their particularity came in part from the grapes being grown in gravelly, well-drained sites, which encouraged even and relatively rapid ripening, and in part from the meticulous attention that ambitious vintners gave them. Before long, Haut-Brion was joined by other estates that remain famous today. With names such as Lafite, Latour, and Margaux, by 1800, these became the most revered wines in the world. Not only did they taste good, but drinking them signaled that one had good taste.

RELATED TOPICS
See also
CABERNET SAUVIGNON & CHÂTEAU LATOUR
page 62

WHY CHAMPAGNE SPARKLES
page 86

BORDEAUX
page 100

3-SECOND BIOGRAPHIES
ARNAUD III DE PONTAC
1599–1681
French owner of Haut-Brion who led the way in creating a new style of Bordeaux wine

SAMUEL PEPYS
1633–1703
English diarist who penned the first tasting note on the new Bordeaux wines

EXPERT
Paul Lukacs

Bordeaux's wines were famous by the Middle Ages, but it was the 1855 classification under Napoleon III that confirmed its status.

WHY CHAMPAGNE SPARKLES

RELATED TOPICS
See also
FERMENTATION
page 32

MAKING CHAMPAGNE
page 40

CLOSURES
page 48

3-SECOND SIP
Making Champagne sparkle became possible following a series of discoveries, starting with the invention of strong glass that allowed wine to continue to ferment in the bottle, trapping its bubbles until the cork is popped.

3-MINUTE TOP OFF
Contrary to legend, French Benedictine monk Dom Pérignon did not invent bubbly Champagne. No single individual did. Dom Pérignon, however, was a master blender. While he made still wines, his insistence on using the right grape varieties in the right proportions was copied by other vintners, including clerics, much later when Champagne finally began to sparkle.

Though grapes had long been cultivated in Champagne in northern France, sparkling wine was invented there over a span of two centuries, beginning in the late 1600s. Fermentation converts sugar into alcohol and carbon dioxide, causing all wines to effervesce; Champagne was created when winemakers were able to trap the bubbles inside the bottle. The first step was the development of sturdy glass bottles and secure stoppers. The second followed the discovery that adding sugar could make the region's tart wines taste richer. The difficulty, however, was knowing how much sugar: too little produced too few bubbles; too much exerted pressure that would break the bottle. But in 1838, a professor invented an instrument to measure the sugar and accurately predict the resultant pressure. Two decades earlier, Champagne Clicquot Ponsardin's cellar master had devised a method of inverting and twisting Champagne bottles—riddling—to remove the yeasty sediment. Then a Belgian inventor developed a process of freezing the neck of the bottle to expel the spent yeast but save the sparkle. Together, these innovations resulted in a wine that exploded in popularity. In 1800, Champagne was producing about 300,000 bottles of frothy wine. A century later, the figure was 30 million; today it is more than 300 million.

3-SECOND BIOGRAPHIES
DOM PIERRE PÉRIGNON
1638–1715
French treasurer of the Abbey of Hautvillers in Champagne, who popularized sparkling wines from that region

ANDRÉ FRANÇOIS
fl. 1836
French professor who invented an instrument for measuring sugar and pressure in sparkling wine

EXPERT
Paul Lukacs

Champagne is not the only wine to sparkle but it has the reputation for being the best, due to its climate, geology, and production method.

A CENTURY OF CRISES

Wine bathed briefly in glory in the nineteenth century. Increased affluence among Europe's expanding middle class brought wines, previously imbibed only by the rich, to a wider public, eager to express their good taste. Beginning in the 1850s, however, wine endured a series of crises. Some were agricultural, others cultural; collectively, they caused wine to plummet in prestige. First came disease—mildews, black rot, and phylloxera, all brought to Europe on American vines. Sprays to combat mildews were developed, and more than 99 percent of the continent's vineyards had to be replanted with resistant rootstocks in response to phylloxera—a process that took nearly two generations for growers to recover. Meanwhile, poor-quality imported wine, much from North Africa and much sold under false labels, flooded the market. Fine wine's reputation was damaged, and drinkers sought an alternative with which to make merry. They found it first in absinthe and other harsh distillates, then in cocktails. Increasingly, winemakers felt under siege; some literally had been in 1914, and would be again in 1939, when war impoverished markets and bombs exploded in vineyards. Shaken, not stirred, wine's fortunes ultimately recovered spectacularly in the second half of the twentieth century.

EXPERT
Paul Lukacs

In the United States in the 1920s, Prohibition and "dry" crusaders meant liquor of dubious provenance were disguised with powerfully flavored mixers and concoctions, such as the Martini, Sidecar, and Gin Fizz, became all the rage.

THE START OF APPELLATIONS

3-SECOND SIP
AOC is France's certification of a wine's quality and a guarantee of its provenance, a system that is also used to classify produce as diverse as cheese, chickens, lentils, and lavender.

3-MINUTE TOP OFF
The first AOC rules were formulated by Pierre Le Roy de Boiseaumarié in 1923, in Châteauneuf-du-Pape in the southern Rhône Valley. He drew the appellation's borders, set minimum alcohol levels, and limited both yields and the varieties permitted. Châteauneuf, previously a source of mostly cheap bulk wines, produces some of France's most prestigious ones.

Wine's return to popularity and prestige after a century of crises began with a return to its roots, literally, with renewed focus on terroir, the unique particularities of "place." A crucial first step was the creation of appellations in France in the 1920s. Individual geographical units were designated as appellations to guarantee the authenticity of any wine made with grapes grown there. Regulations mandated not only where the wine came from but also which varieties went into it and how it had to be made. While keeping some existing practices, others were discarded and new ones were added, compelling vintners who wanted to use appellation names to improve quality. No longer could red Burgundy include cheap wine from southern France, or Bordeaux have barrels of Spanish red in the blend. Everything was legislated, from size of crop to how long the wine was aged. As the initial *Appellation d'origine contrôlée* (controlled designation of origin) or AOC rules decreed, winemakers had to follow "loyal, local, and constant" practices. Similar legislation and appellation systems were instituted in other wine-producing countries during the second half of the century. Although not always as restrictive, they had the cumulative effect of raising quality worldwide and making the label on a wine bottle something that consumers could again trust.

RELATED TOPICS
See also
TERROIR
page 16

MEDIEVAL MONKS
page 82

A CENTURY OF CRISES
page 88

3-SECOND BIOGRAPHIES
JOSEPH CAPUS
1867–1947
French legislator who spearheaded the movement to create controlled appellations throughout France

PIERRE LE ROY DE BOISEAUMARIÉ
1890–1967
French wine estate owner who created France's first official appellation

EXPERT
Paul Lukacs

France's appellation system for quality wines can designate a single vineyard in Burgundy or an entire valley, such as the Loire.

THE JUDGMENT OF PARIS

3-SECOND SIP
The 1976 Paris tasting heralded the emergence of new wines from new places that could compete with Europe's best.

3-MINUTE TOP OFF
The judges at the Paris tasting confused the different wines, ascribing to the Californians attributes such as delicacy and finesse, that they assumed had to be French. At that time, such confusion was the highest compliment one could pay a California wine. Since then, vintners throughout the world have stopped laboring to imitate foreign models and begun to let their own wines assert an identity coming from their native *terroir*.

In May 1976, Steven Spurrier, an Englishman with a wine shop in Paris, organized a wine tasting at the Paris Intercontinental Hotel. Nine eminent French wine professionals gathered to taste and evaluate twenty wines— red Bordeaux, white Burgundies, and some Cabernet Sauvignons and Chardonnays from northern California. None expected the American wines to perform well and the results of the blind tasting shocked everyone. When all twenty wines had been swirled, savored, and spat out, the highest-ranking wine in each category was from Napa Valley; Chardonnay Chateau Montelena 1973 in the whites section and Cabernet Sauvignon Stag's Leap Wine Cellar 1973 in the reds section. Suddenly, California, and by extension all New World wine regions, had to be taken seriously as sources of truly fine wine. Over the next two decades, similar tastings featured wines from Argentina, Australia, Chile, New Zealand, South Africa, and more. While non-European wines did not always win, they continually demonstrated their place in such august company. Modern science in vineyards and wineries, coupled with an investment, had resulted in evermore excellent wines coming from evermore places. By the start of the twenty-first century, the fine-wine map, once confined to western Europe, had become truly global.

RELATED TOPICS
See also
TERROIR
page 16

NAPA VALLEY
page 106

3-SECOND BIOGRAPHIES
WARREN WINIARSKI
1928–
Californian owner and wine, maker at Stag's Leap Wine Cellars, whose Cabernet Sauvignon triumphed in Paris

STEVEN SPURRIER
1941–
British wine merchant who organized the 1976 tasting that would become historic

PIERRE BRÉJOUX
French head of the Institut National des Appellations d'Origine, and chief judge at the Paris tasting

EXPERT
Paul Lukacs

Careers were made and expectations confounded when California's wines triumphed over France's in the 1976 blind tasting.

June 18, 1913
Born in Virginia,
Minnesota

1937
Graduates in economics
from Stanford University
and later begins work at
the Sunnyhill winery in
St. Helena, California

1943
Cesare Mondavi acquires
the Charles Krug Winery
in St. Helena with sons
Robert and Peter

1966
Establishes the Robert
Mondavi Winery with his
two sons on the Oakville
Highway, Napa Valley

1968
Markets the first
Fumé-Blanc, a dry,
oak-aged Sauvignon;
rhe style (and name) was
so successful it was
widely copied, as far
afield as Australia

1968
Releases his first
Cabernet Sauvignon,
a milestone in the Napa
Valley's modern
renaissance

1979
Establishes the Mondavi
Woodbridge Winery in
Lodi, California, to focus
on higher volume,
lower-priced wines

1985
Introduces high-density
plantings of Cabernet
Sauvignon vines to
reduce yields and
maximize fruit
concentration

1989
Selected as *Decanter* Man
of the Year

1995
Creates a joint venture
with Tuscany's Marchesi
de Frescobaldi, producing
several labels, including
Luce and Lucente

2002
Receives the Order of
Merit of the Italian
Republic

2005
Receives the Legion of
Honor from the French
government

2007
Inducted into the
California Hall of Fame

May 16, 2008
Dies just short of his
95th birthday

2008
University of California,
Davis opens The Robert
Mondavi Institute for
Wine and Food Science;
Mondavi had helped
fund it to the tune of
$25 million

ROBERT MONDAVI

Wine maker and philanthropist,
Robert Mondavi was among the most
significant figures in post-Prohibition California
wine. He helped take an industry from the
doldrums to one that could compete
confidently on the world stage. For almost five
decades, he inspired a generation of ambitious
winemakers and introduced millions of
consumers to modern California wine.

Mondavi's big break came in 1943, when his
parents bought the Charles Krug Winery in
St. Helena. Working here with his bother Peter,
he refined his knowledge of winemaking
through experimentation and guidance from
famous oenologist André Tchelistcheff.

During the 1950s, Mondavi became
increasingly focused on the Cabernet Sauvignon
grape that led him, in 1962, to Bordeaux. The
trip heightened his appreciation of fine wine,
fine food, and culture, related themes that were
to feature throughout his later life.

After a bitter dispute with his brother in 1965,
he left the family business and, with his two
sons, established the Napa Valley's first major
new winery for decades. It soon became one of
the most successful in the United States.
Architecturally imposing, "Mission-style" Robert
Mondavi Winery was in the vanguard of
technical and marketing innovation, introducing
temperature-controlled fermentation and
championing the use of French oak barrels.
Mondavi also popularized the now common
practice of selling wine by grape variety.

His unerring belief in Napa's world-class
potential was vindicated in 1976, when local
wines out-performed top ranking Bordeaux
and Burgundy in the landmark tasting known
as the Judgment of Paris (see page 92). The
winning wines were made by Mike Grgich,
wine maker at Chateau Montelena, and Warren
Winiarski, owner-winemaker of Stag's Leap Wine
Cellar, both of whom had previously worked
for Mondavi.

Mondavi's long-held ambition to create an
ultrapremium wine came to fruition in 1979,
after years of discussion with Bordeaux
luminary Baron Philippe de Rothschild. The
Opus One joint venture between their two
families was formally announced in 1980. Its
success inspired other Mondavi partnerships in
Chile with the Chadwick family, and in Tuscany
with the Marchesi de Frescobaldi.

From the 1970s, the Mondavi Winery also
drove Napa Valley's bourgeoning cultural scene,
hosting glamorous events from international
culinary seminars to an acclaimed annual
Summer Music Festival.

Active well into his late eighties, Robert
Mondavi was also prominent in the fight
against America's antialcohol lobby. An iconic
wine patriarch whose legacy lives on, he was
posthumously inducted into the California Hall
of Fame in 2007 by Governor Arnold
Schwarzenegger and First Lady Maria Shriver.

ICONIC REGIONS

1855 Classification A hierarchy of Bordeaux best wine estates drawn up for the Paris Exhibition of 1855. It covered the red wines of the Médoc and the sweet wines of Sauternes-Barsac and was based upon average market prices over many decades. The one geographical exception was the famous Château Haut-Brion, a Premier Cru Classé (First Growth) in the Graves region. The classification has remained intact for more than 150 years, although in 1973, Baron Philippe de Rothschild of Château Mouton-Rothschild was successful in lobbying for his estate to be elevated to First Growth status.

carbonic maceration A method of making red wine starting with whole, uncrushed bunches of grapes. A nonyeast-driven fermentation begins inside each berry in an anaerobic environment converting sugars to alcohol. Carbon dioxide, a by-product of fermentation, eventually causes the grapes to burst, letting fermentation continue in the normal aerobic manner. This is the principle behind wine making in Beaujolais and results in an overtly fruity and supple wine.

claret A uniquely Anglo-Saxon term, originating from the Middle Ages, for the red wines of Bordeaux. At the time, red and white grapes were vinified together, producing a lighter-colored red than is the norm today. The French called it *clairet,* meaning light red.

climat a French term for a specific, often small area of a vineyard with its own distinct terroir. It may be known by its historic name or *lieu-dit.* In Burgundy, *climat* is used as a synonym for vineyard. If it has its own appellation and is wholly owned by a single grower it is called a **monopole**.

Côte-d'Or A French *département*, and the heart of the Burgundy wine region comprising the Côte de Beaune and the Côte de Nuits. Its capital is Beaune.

domaine A French word for a wine-growing estate, especially in Burgundy but also used in other regions of France. In Bordeaux, the more common term for a wine estate is **château,** which may or may not have a grand residence at its center.

Échelle des Crus A system developed in Champagne in the mid-twentieth century to distinguish the quality of grapes grown in different villages and to set prices accordingly (*échelle* means "ladder"). Villages rated

90–99 percent are Premiers Crus while 100 percent-rated villages are Grands Crus. Originally, growers received the corresponding percentage of the declared grapes' price. Today, pricing is more flexible.

First Growths The elite group of five châteaux in the Médoc and Graves regions of Bordeaux ranked Premiers Crus in the 1855 Classification. They are Châteaux Latour, Lafite-Rothschild, Mouton-Rothschild, Margaux, and Haut-Brion.

international varieties Grape varieties that stem from the classic wine regions of Europe and are today grown through the wine-producing world. The top varieties are sometimes referred to as the **noble grapes.** Of the reds, these are Cabernet Sauvignon, Merlot, Pinot Noir, and Syrah/Shiraz. Of the whites, Riesling, Chardonnay, Semillon, Sauvignon Blanc, and Chenin Blanc.

The Médoc The best-known wine district of Bordeaux that extends north of the city and west of the Gironde estuary. It is often referred to as Bordeaux's "Left Bank" and most famously encompasses eight appellations, including the Haut-Médoc communes of Margaux, St. Julien, Pauillac, and St. Estèphe. It was the subject of the **1855 Classification,** still in use today.

Monopole See *Climat*

Premier Cru, Grand Cru The vineyard quality classifications enshrined in French Appellation (AOC) systems, but whose significance varies from region to region. The word *cru* translates as "growth" and can refer to a single vineyard or group of vineyards. On Bordeaux's "Left Bank," the five top wines are called Premiers Crus Classés or First Growths. In St. Emilion, on the Right Bank, the top thirteen wines are known as Premiers Grands Crus Classés, and some sixty-four Grands Crus Classés estates ranked below them. In Burgundy and Champagne, Grand Cru (or "Great Growth") is the top-quality classification, followed by Premier Cru. Alsace has no Premier Cru classification but around 13 percent of its vineyards are classified Grands Crus.

varietal A wine made entirely (or almost entirely, depending on local wine laws) from a single grape variety. The concept was pioneered in California as early as the 1950s, but really gained traction in the 1970s, when Napa Valley winemakers, such as Robert Mondavi, began marketing Cabernet Sauvignon and Chardonnay. Varietal wines soon became the norm in other wine-making countries, especially Australia, New Zealand, and South Africa. A varietal wine is distinct from one named after its region of origin such as Chablis, Burgundy, and Champagne.

BORDEAUX

Bordeaux is arguably the most

famous wine region in the world, located close to the city with the same name on the southwest coast of France. All red Bordeaux wines are given the moniker "claret," and although much everyday claret is made, it is the upper echelons that take the lion's share of attention—whether it's the painstaking analysis over weather conditions each year, its performance as an investment wine, or the influence of American critic Robert Parker on prices. Claret is often defined as being either "Left Bank" or "Right Bank." Although almost never the sole grape of the blend, Cabernet Sauvignon thrives on the gravelly soil of two Left Bank locations; the Médoc, which is north of Bordeaux city, and Graves, south of the city and west of the Garonne River. On the Right Bank, east of the Dordogne River, the heavier clay soil is more suitable for Merlot, often blended with Cabernet Franc. Malbec and Petit Verdot are less popular grapes but can form part of the blends of some red Bordeaux. Dry white Bordeaux is typically a blend of Sauvignon Blanc and Semillon, which, together with Muscadelle, are the varieties used to make Bordeaux's famous sweet wines in subregions, such as Sauternes and Barsac.

RELATED TOPICS

See also
SWEET WINES
page 42

CABERNET SAUVIGNON
& CHÂTEAU LATOUR
page 62

BORDEAUX'S RISE TO
PROMINENCE
page 84

A CENTURY OF CRISES
page 88

THE START OF APPELLATIONS
page 90

EXPERT
Jane Parkinson

3-SECOND SIP
Bordeaux has a long-established reputation as the home of some of the most expensive red and sweet white wines in the world.

3-MINUTE TOP OFF
The 1855 Médoc Classification is Bordeaux's most famous quality hierarchy. It ranks the estates (châteaux) instead of the quality of vineyards and has five levels, classed as "growths." First Growth châteaux are those at the pinnacle and usually command the highest prices. There are five First Growth properties: Mouton-Rothschild, Latour, Lafite-Rothschild, Margaux, and Haut-Brion, the last of which was upgraded (which seldom happens) in 1973/74.

Bordeaux's châteaux are dedicated to making fine wines. Red Cabernet blends dominate production, but white wines, likewise, range from good to sublime.

Château
Mouton Rothschild

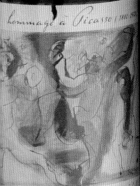

BURGUNDY

3-SECOND SIP
Red Burgundy and
white Burgundy from
the Côte d'Or are widely
regarded as the ultimate
manifestation of Pinot
Noir and Chardonnay,
respectively.

3-MINUTE TOP OFF
The Napoleonic laws of
inheritance, under which
land must be shared
equally among a deceased
person's children, have
greatly contributed to
the Burgundian landscape.
Today, a complicated
patchwork of vineyards
exists, leaving growers to
tend minute plots. This
explains why famous
vineyard names, with their
own appellation such as
Le Montrachet or Le
Chambertin, can be used
by several producers.

Burgundy, the limestone ridge that runs almost north–south in northeast France, is often placed on a pedestal for making benchmark Pinot Noir and Chardonnay, its protagonist varieties. Its most sought-after wines come from the Côte d'Or, which itself is divided in two: Côte de Nuits, where Pinot Noir strongly dominates, and Côte de Beaune, which is more (though not exclusively) Chardonnay territory. Most Burgundy producers are referred to as "domaines," including the most famous property: Domaine de la Romanée-Conti, which makes the most rarified and costly Pinot Noir in the world. Anecdotally, the subregions north and south of the Côte d'Or are at times excluded from being labeled "Burgundy": Chablis in the cool north is the name of the region, the town, and its brisk and racy dry white wine, made purely from Chardonnay. To the south are the Côte Chalonnaise and the Mâconnais, which make recognizably Burgundian red and white wines as well as a softly sparkling version—*crémant de Bourgogne*. Farther south, Beaujolais (unlike Chablis) is officially outside the appellation; its style of wine is entirely different from "red Burgundy," because it is made from the Gamay grape and often undergoes a process called carbonic maceration, which lends Beaujolais a distinctive fruity character.

RELATED TOPICS
See also
PINOT NOIR &
LA ROMANÉE-CONTI
page 64

MEDIEVAL MONKS
page 82

EXPERT
Jane Parkinson

Burgundy is a landscape of small lots of vines that yield some of the most superlative expressions of Pinot Noir and Chardonnay made anywhere on Earth.

TUSCANY

RELATED TOPIC
See also
SWEET WINES
page 42

EXPERT
Jane Parkinson

3-SECOND SIP
Savory, tannic, and tasting of cherries, Sangiovese is Tuscany's best indigenous red-wine variety.

3-MINUTE TOP OFF
Tuscany's most revered and notorious wines are those that broke Italian wine rules back in the 1970s. Producers of expensive wines from nonnative grapes, such as Cabernet Sauvignon and Merlot, had to market them as "declassified," because use of such grapes prohibited them from being included in Italy's wine quality hierarchy until 1992, when a new designation, IGT (*Indicazione Geografica Tipica*), was created for this superlative class of wines. The "Super Tuscans" now rank among the most sought-after wines in the world. Famous—and memorable—names include Ornellaia, Masseto, Sassicaia, and Tignaello.

This celebrated region in central Italy champions one grape above all others for red wine: Sangiovese, the main component of Chianti, Tuscany's most famous wine region. Chianti has two key areas: Chianti Classico, the heart of the region and considered its best part, and Chianti, which is itself divided into seven subregions, all of which can produce enjoyable wines, especially those from the Rufina subregion. On the slopes around the hilly town of Montalcino, where temperatures are hotter than in Chianti, Brunello makes one of Tuscany's signature wines. Intense, tannic, and bold, Brunello di Montalcino usually needs a good decade to soften for optimum drinking. Its earlier-maturing sibling Rosso di Montalcino has courted controversy in recent years (which is now resolved), due to confusion over the grapes included in its blend. Tuscany also makes sweet and dry white wines. Richly flavored Vin Santo is usually made from Trebbiano and Malvasia grapes laid on straw or hung up to air-dry to concentrate the sugars. Tuscany's best dry white wines come from the coast, where the Vermentino grape makes zesty and refreshing whites to quench local thirst.

Italy is blessed with ideal conditions for growing grapes, and, lying at its heart, is Tuscany, whose ancient wine-making pedigree rested on local grapes. Planting international varieties alongside the all-Italian classics has resulted in some remarkable wines.

NAPA VALLEY

3-SECOND SIP
Napa Valley is the United States' most prestigious wine region, especially renowned for its intense Cabernet Sauvignon wines.

3-MINUTE TOP OFF
Set between the Vaca and Mayacamas mountain ranges, Napa experiences great temperature variation, which accounts for significant differences in grape plantings and wine styles along its 30-mile (50 kilometer) strip. Calistoga, its most northerly point, makes Cabernet Sauvignon that is rich and meaty. Here, the average summer temperature is several degrees higher than in Los Carneros down south, which explains why Pinot Noir is Carneros' grape of choice for still and sparkling wines with an enviable reputation.

If wine regions were royalty, Napa Valley would be reigning monarch in California and indeed the United States. Situated 70 miles (112 kilometers) north of San Francisco, Napa's first winery was founded in the second half of the nineteenth century and many followed suit. However, phylloxera and then Prohibition halted its ambitions. In 1966, Robert Mondavi, widely regarded as the region's founding father, opened his winery, swiftly followed by others. Napa staked its place in wine history in 1976, at the so-called Judgment of Paris, a blind tasting held in Paris, when two Napa wines—one white, one red—triumphed over famous French wines in their respective categories. Since then, the region has been transformed into a sophisticated tourist-friendly wine hub. Cabernet Sauvignon is Napa's most cherished and admired grape, especially in the American Viticultural Areas (AVA) of Oakville and Rutherford, where the wines are robust and powerful, the best capable of aging for decades. Red grapes Merlot and Zinfandel are also grown; Pinot Noir is favored in the south; and Chardonnay is easily the most significant white grape. Napa is also home to several of California's "cult" wines, such as Screaming Eagle, Harlan, Araujo, Colgin Cellars, Dalla Valle, and Grace Family.

RELATED TOPICS
See also
CABERNET SAUVIGNON & CHÂTEAU LATOUR
page 62

REGIONAL GRAPES & WINE STYLES
page 74

THE JUDGMENT OF PARIS
page 92

EXPERT
Jane Parkinson

Once seen as a remote fruit-farming district, Napa Valley is now the symbol as well as the heart of California's top-quality wine production.

RIOJA

South of Bilbao, Rioja is the
region of northern-central Spain that until
recently was considered the exclusive source
of the country's best red wines; today, it
shares that reputation with Ribera del Duero
and Priorat. Rioja straddles the Ebro River as it
heads southeast from Haro, spanning an area
so vast it is subdivided into three zones: Rioja
Alta, Rioja Alavesa, and Rioja Baja. Rioja follows
a hierarchy that stipulates minimum aging
periods of the wine, both in barrel and bottle.
The higher the quality of the wine, the longer
it is aged. In descending order, this ranking
runs Gran Reserva, Reserva, Crianza, and Rioja,
although a new wave of quality producers
has tended to disregard that classification.
Tempranillo is the chief grape used in red
Rioja, although as a style that is typically
blended; Garnacha is also of huge importance.
Graciano and Mazuelo (Carignan) are common
components of red Rioja, albeit to a lesser
extent, while Cabernet Sauvignon has also taken
root here. Red Rioja's most famous producer is
Marqués de Murrieta Castillo Ygay. White Rioja
is often—and unfairly—overlooked: it is usually
made from a blend of local white grapes: Viura,
Malvasia Riojana, and/or Garnacha Blanca.

3-SECOND SIP
A name that is familiar
and appreciated around
the world, Rioja is a
Spanish region of
considerable reputation,
making everything from
everyday wines to some of
the country's most prized.

3-MINUTE TOP OFF
The style of red Rioja has
been a constant source
of debate and discussion.
Historically, red Rioja was
made using American oak
barrels, imparting a telltale
vanilla character to the
wine. In the last twenty
years, wine making has
been tweaked and French
oak became popular,
producing "modern Rioja,"
which is fruitier and darker
than traditional red Rioja.
Today, as producers try to
reauthenticate red Rioja,
American barrels are back
in favor.

RELATED TOPICS
See also
MAKING RED WINE
page 38

ÉLEVAGE
page 46

TEMPRANILLO &
RIBERA DEL DUERO
page 70

EXPERT
Jane Parkinson

*To outsiders, red Rioja
once was the Spanish
wine: full-bodied,
light-hued, and heavily
oaked, which gives a
marked vanilla flavor.
These days, the blend is
smoother, fruitier, and
more delicately oaked.*

STELLENBOSCH

The traditional hub of South

Africa's best-quality wines, Stellenbosch, is 28 miles (45 kilometers) east of Cape Town. The district is steeped in history and renowned for its characteristic settler architecture—white-painted Cape Dutch buildings dot a landscape blanketed with vineyards. The best Stellenbosch wines are often said to come from regions closest to the quaint university town of the same name, where cooling coastal breezes off False Bay delay ripening, generating a desirable lengthier process of maturation for the grapes. Stellenbosch favors the production of red over white wine these days, although excellent white wines are produced— especially from the vines on soil (which varies greatly in the region) that is lighter and sandier—and are chiefly made using Chenin Blanc, Sauvignon Blanc, or Chardonnay. Red Stellenbosch wines are made as varietals or blends—often called Cape Blends. Red grapes that prosper include Cabernet Sauvignon, Shiraz, Merlot, and Pinotage (a variety distinctive to South Africa, created in Stellenbosch University, partly in response to the deadly phylloxera that took hold here at the turn of the twentieh century). Several of South Africa's most revered wine estates are based in Stellenbosch, including Vergelegen, Meerlust, Jordan, Warwick, Simonsberg, and Neil Ellis.

3-SECOND SIP
One of South Africa's oldest wine districts, Stellenbosch is a melting pot of high-quality producers making some of the country's finest red wines.

3-MINUTE TOP OFF
South Africa splits its wine regions into districts that have subzones known as "wards." Those in the Stellenbosch district are Banghoek, Bottelary, Devon Valley, Jonkershoek Valley, Papegaaiberg, Polkadraai Hills, and Simonsberg-Stellenbosch, the last of which was the first to gain official recognition as a Stellenbosch ward.

RELATED TOPICS
See also
PHYLLOXERA
page 24

REGIONAL GRAPES & WINE STYLES
page 74

EXPERT
Jane Parkinson

International varieties, including Cabernet Sauvignon, Merlot, Chenin Blanc, and Chardonnay, feature prominently in blends from Stellenbosch. This region is also famous for Pinotage (a cross between Pinot Noir and Cinsaut), a grape unique to South Africa that makes typically dark-hued wine with pronounced berry and licorice flavors.

MARLBOROUGH

Located on the northeastern tip of South Island, Marlborough is New Zealand's biggest wine region. Its name in Maori means "the place with the hole in the cloud," in reference to the intense sunshine. Sauvignon Blanc rules here. Although Montana was the first winery to commercially plant the grape, its success is largely attributed to one producer, Cloudy Bay, which released an exotic-tasting Sauvignon with an evocative label back in the 1980s. The style was not difficult to replicate, and soon a sea of Marlborough Sauvignon Blanc that tasted of liquid passion fruit was made and remains in huge demand today. If Marlborough's economy has thrived on making this style of wine, its relationship with Sauvignon Blanc is a source of pride and increasing frustration, as Marlborough strives to prove it isn't merely a one-trick pony. This has manifested itself variously, from putting Sauvignon Blanc in oak barrels to producing a longer-lived, food-friendlier style, and making high-class Chardonnay. Today, vineyard capacity is close to its limit, due to lack of land and tighter control over water rights, while sustainable wine making is a key initiative for the whole industry.

3-SECOND SIP
Marlborough is the region that put New Zealand wine on the map.

3-MINUTE TOP OFF
The price of Marlborough Sauvignon Blanc has been a hot topic recently, following some high-yielding vintages, that generated the nickname "Savalanche" for the beginning of harvest. This volume drove prices down, and although it is being corrected, it was a bitter pill to swallow for a region and country that from the outset has commanded higher-than-average prices for its wine in general.

RELATED TOPICS
See also
MAKING WHITE WINE
page 36

ÉLEVAGE
page 46

SAUVIGNON BLANC &
POUILLY FUMÉ
page 60

3-SECOND BIOGRAPHY
KEVIN JUDD
Founding winemaker at Cloudy Bay who produced 25 vintages of its flagship Sauvignon Blanc

EXPERT
Jane Parkinson

The difference in Marlborough's day and night temperatures provides optimum conditions for growing Sauvignon and other aromatic white grapes— Riesling, Pinot Gris, Gewurztraminer, and Grüner Veltliner—while Pinot Noir is the red grape of choice.

BAROSSA VALLEY

RELATED TOPICS
See also
RIESLING &
SCHARZHOF BERGER
page 58

SYRAH/SHIRAZ & HERMITAGE
page 66

REGIONAL GRAPES & WINE
STYLES
page 74

3-SECOND SIP
Barossa Valley is the engine room of Australia's most revered red wines, especially those made from Shiraz.

3-MINUTE TOP OFF
The terms "Barossa Valley" and "Barossa" are frequently and incorrectly used interchangeably. Barossa Valley wines are made exclusively from the valley's fruit, whereas wines labeled "Barossa" can be a blend of grapes from Barossa Valley and its neighboring region Eden Valley, which is famous for Shiraz and Riesling.

Less than 40 miles (60 kilometers) northeast of Adelaide, Barossa Valley is the powerhouse of Australia's top red wines. The vineyards, founded largely by German settlers from Silesia in Prussia are divided by the North Para River. In Barossa's hot and arid climate, Cabernet Sauvignon and Shiraz thrive. Old bush vines of Shiraz, some of them more than a century old, impart an inimitable complexity to the wines on account of their great age. They are the reason for the deservedly iconic status and global reputation of Barossa Shiraz. The best of these wines are rarely at their drinking peak in youth. The sweet black-currant fruit, dense chocolate flavors, and hefty tannins demand this wine to be kept for a minimum of five years—and often more—before blossoming into perfect condition. Barossa Valley makes serious red wines from other Mediterranean varieties, too, including Grenache and Mourvèdre (or Mataro in Australia), and, when blended with Shiraz, they formulate the popular GSM blended red wines. Semillon and Chardonnay are the most popular grapes used to make white wines, some of which can be as complex as the reds. Famous producers in this blessed region of South Australia include Penfolds, Wolf Blass, and Jacob's Creek, although the number of quality-obsessed boutique producers seems to be increasing.

EXPERT
Jane Parkinson

Australia's wine capital is one of its oldest wine-growing regions and perhaps the best-known new world wine region, aside from California's Napa Valley. Barossa is synonymous with red gutsy wines, typically made from Grenache, Shiraz, and Mourvèdre.

MENDOZA

Argentina's foremost wine region

lies in the rain shadow of the snow-capped Andes. Accounting for more than two-thirds of Argentina's total wine production, Mendoza has adopted the French red-wine grape Malbec so effectively that its name is almost synonymous with the country, despite the importance of other varieties, including Cabernet Sauvignon and Bonarda for red wines, and, for whites, Chardonnay and Sauvignon Blanc. (Torrontes, Argentina's signature white grape, is more at home in Salta than Mendoza.) Key to Mendoza's success are high altitude—crucial to temper the region's otherwise searing heat and provide a climatic (therefore wine) consistency from year to year—and drying winds off the Andes, which lessen the risk of molds and rot. Thanks to a nineteenth-century French immigrant who first planted Malbec in Mendoza, this disease-prone, frost-sensitive grape successfully took root under the Andes. The Uco Valley is currently one of Mendoza's most heralded subregions, producing exquisite full-bodied Malbecs rich in black fruit and spice. Unusually, the valley is not named after a river but the person who introduced irrigation to this arid region. At its northernmost end, Tupungato is the subregion where some of Mendoza's best Chardonnay is produced.

RELATED TOPICS
See also
PHYLLOXERA
page 24

BORDEAUX'S RISE TO PROMINENCE
page 84

3-SECOND BIOGRAPHY
DOMINGO F. SARMIENTO
1811–88
Argentinian governor of San Juan who instructed a French agronomist to plant French vine cuttings in Mendoza

EXPERT
Jane Parkinson

3-SECOND SIP
With over three-quarters of the world's acreage of Malbec, Mendoza has restored the grape as one of the top varieties for full-bodied red wine.

3-MINUTE TOP OFF
Mendoza's wine industry owes its success to the expertise of European immigrants escaping the scourge of phylloxera and to the skill of the indigenous Huarpe population, who created an intricate canal system that channeled the meltwater from the Andes, irrigating Mendoza sufficiently to grow grapes in a desert.

Mountain influences and bountiful sunshine mean Mendoza enjoys a long growing season (important for wine grapes to develop complexity of flavor), with the fruit retaining fresh acidity while achieving optimum maturity.

September 1941
Born in Barcelona, Spain

1962
Graduates in Oenology
and Viticulture from
Dijon and takes over
at his family's winery

1966
Pioneers planting
international grape
varieties in Spain

1975
Begins experimenting
with organic viticulture

1977
Publishes his first book
Vines and Wines

1979
Torres' 1970 Gran Coronas
Reserva beats Château
Latour 1970 and a host of
other top Cabernet-based
wines at the Gault-Millau
Wine Olympiad in Paris

1979
Establishes Torres as
the first foreign wine
producer in Chile, where
it now produces 4 million
bottles annually

1982
His sister Marimar plants
first U.S. vineyard

1993
Marimar Estate Winery
opens in California

1996
Chilean Government
awards Torres Order of
Bernardo O'Higgins
(grado de gran oficial),
in recognition of his
contribution to Chile's
viticultural development

1997
Establishes joint venture
in China, the Zhangjiakou
Great Wall Torres Winery
Co. Ltd, and a wholesale
and retail wine business,
Torres China

1999
Wine Spectator magazine
declares Torres The Most
Important Winery in
Spain

2001
Torres is the sole Spanish
winery listed in *Wine
Spectator*'s 25th
anniversary Hall of Fame

2002
Named *Decanter*'s "Man
of the Year"

2005
Named *Wine
International* magazine's
"Personality of the Year"

2006
Receives Lifetime
Achievement Award from
Wein Gourmet magazine

2006
Torres named Best
European Winery by *Wine
Enthusiast* magazine

2012
Fifth-generation Miguel
Torres Maczassek takes
over from his father as
Managing Director of
Bodegas Torres SA

2014
Torres named World's
Most Admired Wine
Brand by *Drinks
International*

MIGUEL A. TORRES

Miguel A. Torres is the fourth- generation President of a family-owned company founded by Jaime Torres in 1870 in Penedès, Catalonia. Miguel introduced to Spain modern vinification methods and grape varieties that transformed the image of Spanish wines abroad and made the Torres name synonymous with top-quality.

Miguel studied oenology and viticulture in Dijon, France, and joined the company in 1962, to embark on an impressive wine-making career driven by experimentation, innovation, and achievement.

As early as 1966, he began to plant international varieties, such as Chardonnay and Cabernet Sauvignon, while remaining equally committed to Catalonia's little-known indigenous grape varieties. By 1970, he was using stainless steel tanks with temperature control to produce wines that were fresh, vibrant, fruity in style— revolutionary in Spain at the time. In 1975, ahead of the mainstream, he began experimenting with organic viticulture.

In 1979, the Torres name made headlines when, at the *Gault-Millau* Wine Olympiad in Paris, the Torres Gran Coronas Black Label 1970 (now called Mas La Plana), outscored top Cabernet-based wines, including Bordeaux's Châteaux Latour and Haut-Brion.

That year Torres became the first foreign wine company to set up in Chile. Modern wine-making equipment and new oak barrels brought startling results, which highlighted the country's potential and marked the start of a new era for Chilean wine. It is typical of Miguel Torres' ethical and forward-thinking character that he chose then to pay his Chilean workers four times the going rate, which he calculated to be the minimum required for a decent standard of living. Today, Torres' Chilean winery is a certified organic and Fair Trade producer.

On the death of his father in 1991, Miguel became President and Managing Director. Today, the company has wineries in several Denomination of Origin (DO) regions outside its native Penedès, including Priorat, Ribera del Duero, Toro, Jumilla, and La Rioja as well as ventures in California and China. It spends $3.5 million (more than €3 million) a year on viticultural and wine-making research and has invested in higher, cool vineyards in the foothills of the Pyrenees to mitigate effects of global warming and delay fruit maturation.

In the marketing of wine, he believes focusing on brand instead of region or grape variety is the most effective way to compete with New World producers. Fittingly, in 2014, Torres was named the World's Most Admired Wine Brand by "Drinks International," following a comprehensive industry poll of the world's best-regarded wines.

EMERGING ECONOMIES

RELATED TOPIC
See also
WINE INVESTMENT
page 136

EXPERT
Jane Parkinson

A culmination of modern influences—from outside investment to advanced technology—has placed the wines of emerging countries on the world's table. High on the list is Brazil, where historically high humidity meant the grapes grown were obscure hybrids that could withstand these inclement conditions. However, significant progress has been made in Brazil's top region, Rio Grande do Sul, especially with its most promising style to date: sparkling. Farther north, and closer to the equator, is Vale do São Francisco, a source of fascination for growers in classic wine countries because here the semiarid tropical conditions enable vines to produce two harvests a year. Across the Pacific, Asian countries, too, are improving wine quality, while determining the most suitable styles and/or grape varieties. Significant investment in China—for now more famous as a consumer than producer—combined with the arrival of foreign winemakers has endorsed its potential, in particular, in Shandong province in the east and Ningxia in the west. In India, Maharashtra is currently the most productive wine region, although wine production is flourishing everywhere thanks to government incentives, outside investment, and a booming middle class eager to imbibe.

3-SECOND SIP
Far from the wine grape's natural home, a raft of countries is now making significant strides in quality wine making.

3-MINUTE TOP OFF
Growing grapes for wine on the American continent began in Mexico before spreading to Chile, Argentina, and California. Spanish conquistadors took their love of wine to Mexico, which boasts the Americas' oldest winery, Casa Madero, founded in 1597. Until Mexico's independence, local demand was quenched with imports from Spain after Carlos II outlawed wine making in the colony to protect the Spanish wine industry. Guadalupe Valley is widely tipped to be Mexico's hotspot for quality wine, although styles vary greatly thanks to a melting pot of grape varieties.

Making wine is now a global industry, and consumers accustomed to claret, Californian, or Chilean wine are now able to sample the increasingly impressive output of countries without wine in their cultural tradition.

THE BUSINESS OF WINE

broker A middleman between winegrowers and or merchants and customers. A broker may collect wine samples direct from the producer and present them to merchants, taking a small percentage of any sale (see **courtier**). Fine wine brokers deal in fine and rare vintages, selling wine to merchants and private customers. They may sell their own stock, typically still in its original wooden case under bond, or simply facilitate a sale between a seller and a buyer for a commission.

cave coopérative A cooperative winery owned by a group of local grape growers. They usually produce their own brands but also smaller *cuvées* for individual growers. Advantages include economies of scale and the opportunity for smaller growers, who might not otherwise be able to afford the wine-making infrastructure, to market their own wine.

caviste The French term for a specialty wine retailer.

courtier A French term for a broker who acts as a middleman between winegrowers and or merchants and customers. A broker may collect wine samples direct from the producer and present them to merchants, taking a small percentage of any sale. A *courtier* often specializes in the wines of one region.

en primeur A wine trade term also known as prerelease. It refers to the selling of wine before it has been bottled and released to the market. It has been a traditional way for wine merchants to secure a share of a Bordeaux, Burgundy, or Rhône vintage, and in the late twentieth century the opportunity was extended to consumers. It is particularly popular in instances where demand will probably exceed supply. The buyer pays the opening or "cellar door" price, and at some point, up to two years later, pays the shipping, duty, and any applicable sales tax before taking delivery of the wine. These days, en primeur markets exist around the world, wherever there is a perceived shortage of a particular wine.

evolution (of wine) Wine is constantly evolving. In the winery, the process can be slowed by storing newly made wine in an inert, air-tight, temperature-controlled stainless steel tank until bottling. Wines aged in barrels evolve more quickly due to greater exposure to air. Once bottled, wine has little contact with air other than what is inside the bottle and the minuscule amount that enters through the cork over many years. Evolution in bottle is therefore anaerobic, especially if the bottle is sealed with an airtight Stelvin closure (screw cap). Fine wine often benefits from evolving in bottle. White wines deepen in color over time, while red wines become lighter and the tannins soften. Primary characteristics, such as fruitiness, gradually give way to evolved, complex, nuanced flavors.

Ideal long-term cellaring conditions are a cool, constant (53.6–57.2°F/ 12–14°C) temperature and a slightly humid environment free from direct light and vibration for one to fifty years. Bottles should be laid horizontally to prevent the cork from drying out and the wine leaking.

First Growths The elite group of châteaux in the Médoc and Graves regions of Bordeaux ranked Premiers Crus in the official 1855 Classification. They are Châteaux Latour, Lafite-Rothschild, Mouton-Rothschild, Margaux, and Haut-Brion.

flying winemaker One who makes wine in more than one country, typically a southern hemisphere vintage (January–March), followed by a northern hemisphere vintage (August–October). The term was coined by retail wine merchant Tony Laithwaite who, in the 1980s, brought in cutting-edge Australian and New Zealand winemakers to underperforming, old-fashioned, and often unhygienic cellars in eastern Europe to raise standards and make wine that would be more appealing to the British palate. The concept was taken up by other merchants and grocery stores, especially for store-brand wines, and became mainstream. Today's flying winemakers are just as likely to be European and found working in New World wineries.

in bond (IB) A wine held in a controlled warehouse and on which no duty has yet been paid. For investment purposes, fine wines often change hands many times while still in bond.

MW (Master of Wine) One who has passed the practical and written examinations held annually by the Institute of Masters of Wine. The MW is the wine trade's most demanding professional qualification. The first six MWs qualified in 1953. By 2014, there were still only 319 MWs worldwide. In many countries, there are also official associations of sommeliers with their own qualifications, such as **Master Sommelier (MS)**. They also enter exams and competitions, not least one for the prestigious title of Meilleur Sommelier du Monde, World's Best Sommelier.

négociant The French term for a wholesale wine merchant who buys grapes, must, or young wine in bulk from growers and then makes or blends and bottles it for sale under the négociant's wine label. Examples include Calvet in Bordeaux and Bouchard Père et Fils in Burgundy. Some négociants also make wine from their own vineyards.

PRODUCERS

RELATED TOPIC
See also
WINE INVESTMENT
page 136

3-SECOND SIP
From one-man bands to superscale corporate businesses, wine producers, like wine bottles, come in all shapes and sizes.

3-MINUTE TOP OFF
The term "estate bottled" and its equivalent "*mis en bouteille à la propriété*" (or "*au château*") indicate wine made and bottled on the estate by the grower—normally a superior product. Grocery stores' own brands are frequently supplied by cooperatives, which offer consistently good quality, and many are a beacon of quality for their respective regions.

Although the word "*château*" — or *schloss* or *castello*—is synonymous with fine wines, only a small proportion of modern wines comes from such properties. Bordeaux *châteaux* allocate production via trusted courtiers, who typically make 2 percent on the sale. Courtiers allocate to négociants, who make 10–15 percent. It's a complex web but ensures distribution is fair, and none can blame the Bordeaux *châteaux* if their allocation is modest. Most wine, however—particularly Burgundy—is made on the property by small growers, or domaines, producing a few thousand cases, enough to make a crust. Frequently, however, throughout France, Italy, Spain, and elsewhere, growers sell grapes, not wine. Often they are contracted to one winemaker who will specify vine-training techniques, yields, harvest times, etc. Much of Australia's production relies on such growers. Cooperatives, on the other hand, are owned by growers, perhaps numbering hundreds, who operate on terms such as grape variety and ripeness, not simply quantity. They can afford the equipment, oenologists, and marketing muscle of which the lone grower can only dream, and many coops produce first-rate wines at modest prices.

3-SECOND BIOGRAPHIES
BARON JAMES DE ROTHSCHILD
1792–1868
German-French banker who established the French branch of the Rothschild family

LOUIS GAMBERT DE LOCHE
1884–1967
French vineyard owner who founded the Rhône Cave de Tain coop in 1933 and helped to establish appellation system

PETER LEHMANN
1930–2013
Australian producer who saved growers from ruin by buying grapes his employer had refused, establishing Barossa icon Peter Lehmann Wines

EXPERT
Martin Campion

Fairy-tale castles feature in Bordeaux, the Loire, Rheingau, and Tuscany; more widely, producers are individuals or companies who dwell in ordinary houses.

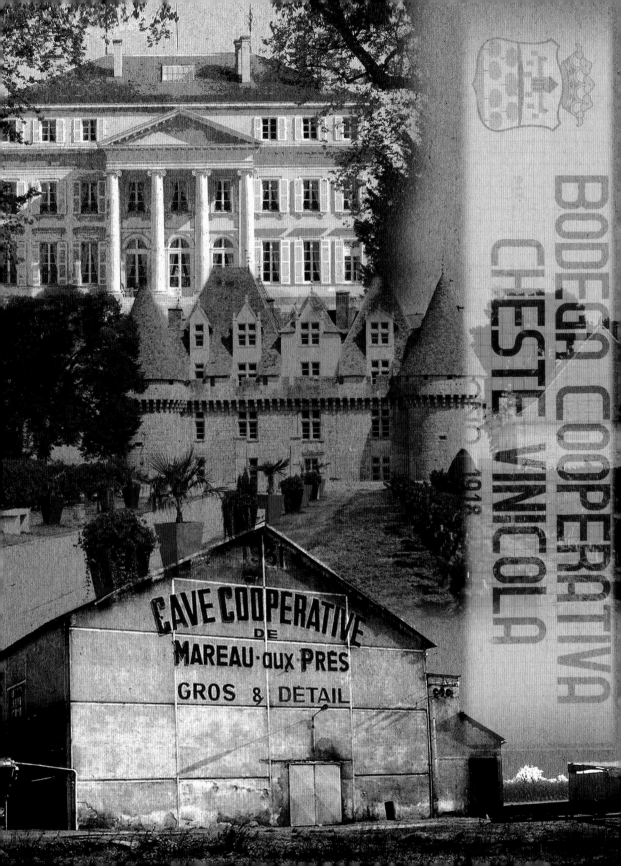

AGENTS, BROKERS & WINE MERCHANTS

3-SECOND SIP
Two decades ago, wine merchants were known for liking long lunches and Savile Row suits; today, they are appreciated entirely for their business acumen, not their appearance.

3-MINUTE TOP OFF
Berry Bros. & Rudd, the archetypal traditional wine merchant, was established in London's St. James's in 1698. With two royal warrants, leather-bound ledgers, and even a letter from White Star Line confirming the loss of 69 cases on board RMS *Titanic*, one almost expects to hear the quiver of quill pens instead of the clatter of keyboards. Yet when its website launched in 1994, it was hailed as the Gold Standard and remains at the cutting edge of wine retailing.

It is estimated wine production

will hit 550 million gallons (25 million hectoliters) by 2016, with a value of U.S. $300 billion. Competition is fierce, and few producers have the resources to sell on a global scale. A top-notch agent who represents a winery beyond the local market is worth their weight in wine, developing detailed knowledge of customers' needs, responding to trends, and allocating sought-after wines across myriad retailers and restaurants. Since the 1990s, the significant rise in fine wine prices, and new wealth in countries such as Russia and China, has seen wine broking flourish. Wine brokers may act as importers for small, select producers, while simultaneously buying from, and selling to, fine wine enthusiasts. Many are active in the annual *en primeur* campaigns for Bordeaux and Burgundy—building a relationship with a broker can be the way to acquire a few precious bottles of a rare wine. A good merchant or wholesaler may combine all these roles: sourcing direct from handpicked estates, buying from agents and brokers, and acting as brokers themselves, selling clients' wines to other clients or to other brokers. In such a competitive market, it pays to establish a USP, such as Burgundy, California, or Champagne.

RELATED TOPICS
See also
RETAILERS
page 130

WINE INVESTMENT
page 136

3-SECOND BIOGRAPHIES
SIMON BERRY
1957–
Chairman of Berry Bros & Rudd and Clerk to the Royal Cellars

STEPHEN BROWETT
1959–
Chairman and owner of world-renowned winebroker Farr Vintners, founded in 1978

EXPERT
Martin Campion

Selling wine, like any other commodity, can be a local affair, conducted from the cellar door or, more likely, involve a chain of professionals to reach the global market.

RETAILERS

Fine wine is no longer the preserve of emperors, top university professors, and the alumni of Harvard: it is within the reach of ordinary people—so much so that grocery stores represent many of take-home sales. Retailers, such as upscale Waitrose, have several MWs on their team and most have their own "flying winemakers," whose experience and knowledge of customer preferences have helped to improve quality and drive sales. Frequently, they are spearheading wine-drinking trends. Tesco, one of the world's largest retailers, sells about 10 percent of all Marlborough Sauvignon Blanc, and many, including Costco, sell substantial quantities of Bordeaux Grands Crus at competitive prices. Yet there remains room for the independent specialist, the lone *caviste*, whose *raison d'être* is not to compete on price, but to truffle out gems from small producers who hold little interest for volume-hungry grocery stores. London's Hedonism is a prime—perhaps extreme—example. With staff collectively speaking fifteen languages and a range of more than 7,000 products, it has the lot: simple wines at a modest $10 (£8) a bottle to those requiring a banker's bonus, such as Krug 1966, Yquem 1811, and Penfolds 2004 Block 42 Ampoule—one of only twelve—a snip at $150,000 (£120,000) per bottle.

3-SECOND SIP
Chain store retailers have changed the face of wine buying—and wine drinking—forever, placing wine alongside the weekly groceries.

3-MINUTE TOP OFF
Grocery stores often charge an artificially high price, only to slash it in a buy-one-get-one-free offer. Superficially, this looks good for canny customers, but not for the humble grape grower. Few live in the opulent châteaux common to the elite of Bordeaux; fewer still can afford to turn down the grocery store chain looking for a deal. The result? Perfectly drinkable yet bland wines, made to please the purse more readily than the palate.

RELATED TOPICS
See also
AGENTS, BROKERS
& WINE MERCHANTS
page 126

WINE & FOOD
page 148

3-SECOND BIOGRAPHIES
JAMES SINEGAL &
JEFFREY H. BROTMAN
1936– & 1943–
American founders of Costco, one of the world's largest wine retailers, in 1983

TONY LAITHWAITE
1941–
English cofounder (with wife Barbara) of UK wine retailer Laithwaite's and the Sunday Times Wine Club

YEVGENY CHICHVARKIN
1974–
Russian cell phone tycoon and founder of Hedonism Wines in 2012

EXPERT
Martin Campion

Wine is now accepted as part of the culture in much of the Westernized world.

SOMMELIERS

For a long time, sommeliers had a reputation for being lofty figures, steeped in fine wine since birth, and hardly the most approachable of restaurant staff. Dressed in a long black apron and black jacket, decorated with a silver or gold brooch shaped like a bunch of grapes to signify the wine connection, sommeliers could easily make diners feel uncomfortable or—worse—inferior when selecting wine. Fortunately, the profession has advanced considerably, and diners now feel more freely able to talk to sommeliers, usually less somberly dressed, about the wine(s) to accompany their meal, without risking humiliation. Sommeliers need to be versatile; their job encompasses far more than opening and serving wine. In order to describe and recommend a wine, they must have extensive wine and food knowledge and be excellent tasters. However, they must also be commercially savvy to buy wines intelligently and price them well—competent sommeliers will be as adroit with accounting formulas and spreadsheets as corkscrews. And they require a healthy dose of psychology to capture the emotions of customers and understand correctly the type of occasion the diners are coming to experience. All that wrapped in a great sense of hospitality to ensure guests will return again and again to renew the pleasure.

3-SECOND SIP
The sommelier is the person charged with purchasing, recommending, and serving wine in a restaurant.

3-MINUTE TOP OFF
Competitions to become the top sommelier exist at national, continental, and international levels, including the truly global "Best Sommelier of the World," and are avidly contested by large numbers of sommeliers. For a long time, sommellerie was a male-dominated trade, but young women are increasingly assuming the role with great aplomb. A U.S. documentary, *Somm* (2012), about the Master Sommelier examination, rapidly became a cult movie.

RELATED TOPICS
See also
HOW TO TASTE
page 146

WINE & FOOD
page 148

3-SECOND BIOGRAPHY
PAUL BRUNET
1935–
French Master Sommelier, author, and doyen of the sommellerie trade

EXPERT
Gerard Basset OBE

Intimate knowledge of wine and food matches, professional service, and a sense of occasion are the hallmarks of the top sommeliers.

WINE WRITERS, JOURNALISTS & CRITICS

3-SECOND SIP
The public's thirst for knowledge is now quenched by an outpouring of wine publications and expert opinion.

3-MINUTE TOP OFF
First-century naturalist Pliny the Elder (23–79 CE) authored the thirty-seven-volume encyclopaedia *Naturalis Historia*; book 14 deals exclusively with wine, including a ranking of the First Growths of Rome, and book 17 includes viticultural techniques and the concept of terroir. In his ranking of the best Roman wines, he concludes the vineyard has more influence than grape variety on the finished wine, a view shared by most modern experts.

"*In vino veritas*," Pliny the Elder famously remarked—"in wine there is truth." Pliny and fellow Roman Virgil wrote much on wine, while Greek historian Thucydides referred to the civilizing effect of vine cultivation. Long after those ancient worthies first scribed on the topic, Edmund Penning-Rowsell, Pamela Vandyke-Price, and Harry Waugh laid the foundations for modern wine writing. For many, Hugh Johnson, author of the *Pocket Wine Book*, *The Story of Wine,* and *The World Atlas of Wine*, is the greatest living wine writer, closely followed by fellow author, journalist, and critic Jancis Robinson, whose website has global influence. Wine, like food, has become a standard feature of weekend newspapers, and a glowing review can be enough to strip the grocery-store shelves. *Wine Magazine* became the annual International Wine Challenge, while *Decanter* holds its World Wine Awards, both judged by winemakers, writers, sommeliers, and buyers/sellers, and a medal from either indicates a standout wine. *Wine Spectator*, which organizes yearly Fine Wine Encounters with the world's finest producers, holds significant sway in the United States. None has been more influential than the critic Robert M. Parker. For many, 100 points from RP are the holy grail, frequently guaranteeing a sell-out vintage.

RELATED TOPICS
See also
TERROIR
page 16

WINE'S SPIRITUAL BEGINNINGS
page 80

RETAILERS
page 130

3-SECOND BIOGRAPHIES
HUGH JOHNSON OBE
1939 –
English author of international best-selling wine books

MARVIN SHANKEN MBA
1943 –
American publisher of the *Wine Spectator*

JANCIS ROBINSON MW
1950–
English author of best-selling wine books, influential blogger, and first nonwine trade MW

EXPERT
Martin Campion

Wine books, blogs, and websites have done much to bring the noble beverage within the reach of ordinary people.

WINE INVESTMENT

Obey a few simple rules and investing in wine can be enormously rewarding. Buying *en primeur* guarantees provenance and lets buyers select bottle sizes, although rare wines can be impossible to obtain without significant outlay on lesser wines, or substantial expenditure on other rarities. A case of top Bordeaux, such as 1990 Lafite, could be bought for about $640 *en primeur*, yet today stands around $12,000 at auction; the 1982 (cost $380) at nearly $31,000 (from a high of $84,000). Storing under bond saves money and guarantees the watchful eye of customs officials, which lessens the chance of the wine being a fake (a growing problem at auctions, although increasingly well policed). Bordeaux's dominance is diminishing slightly with top Burgundies soaring (2005 DRC has doubled to nearly $15,000 per bottle over the last few years) and other regions, such as Champagne and Italy's Piedmont, showing fine returns. Shrewd investors buy the best they can afford from a well-reputed merchant and store with a specialist, such as world-renowned Octavian Cellars. If storing with the merchant, marking the investor's name literally on the case is the way to avoid them becoming one of many creditors in the event the merchant collapses.

3-SECOND SIP
Fine wine, like art, can be a good, relatively low risk, long-term investment.

3-MINUTE TOP OFF
Such has been Chinese interest in Bordeaux that, to paraphrase Victor Kiam's Remington ads from the 1980s, they bought the châteaux. It's estimated China had invested in more than sixty properties by 2014, and not only in Bordeaux; in July 2014, the Chinese company 1847 Winery bought Château Yaldara in Australia's Barossa Valley. Investment flows in the other direction, too; the Rothschilds of Lafite have planted more than 60 acres (25 hectares) with Chinese partner CITIC, in the Penglai peninsula.

RELATED TOPICS
See also
AGENTS, BROKERS & WINE MERCHANTS
page 128

WINE WRITERS, JOURNALISTS & CRITICS
page 134

ROBERT M. PARKER
page 138

3-SECOND BIOGRAPHIES
MICHAEL BROADBENT MW
1927–
English expert on wine, author, and Head of Christie's Wine Department until 2009

SERENA SUTCLIFFE MW
1945–
English expert on Champagne and Bordeaux, author, Head of Wine at Sotheby's, and former rival to Michael Broadbent on the London auction scene

EXPERT
Martin Campion

It's wise to invest in what you enjoy: liquid assets are a palatable alternative to buying stocks and shares.

July 23, 1947
Born Baltimore, Maryland

1967
Visits Alsace, his first introduction to French wines

1970
Makes his inaugural trip to the Rhône Valley

1973
Graduates in law from the University of Maryland

1978
Sends out complimentary issue of his wine journal, *The Baltimore/Washington Wine Advocate*

1983
Attracts wider attention following his resounding endorsement of Bordeaux's 1982 vintage, now acknowledged as one of the best of the century

1984
Retires from the Farm Credit Banks of Baltimore to devote himself entirely to writing his bimonthly *Wine Advocate*

1985
Publishes *The Wine Buyer's Guide to Bordeaux*

1986
Establishes, with his brother-in-law, Michael Etzel, a vineyard/winery in Oregon—Beaux Frères

1987
Publishes *The Wines of the Rhône Valley and Provence*, followed, in 1990, by *Burgundy*

1993
French President François Mitterrand makes him a Chevalier dans l'Ordre National du Mérite for services to French wine abroad

1999
French President Jacques Chirac promotes Parker to Chevalier dans l'Ordre de la Légion d'Honneur

1997
Publishes *Wines of the Rhône Valley* (2nd ed.)

1998
Wine Advocate subscriptions reach 45,000 in thirty-five countries and the French language edition is launched

2002
Online version of erobertparker.com goes live, and is now the world's most-visited wine information website

2002
Made a Commendatore dell'Ordine al Merito della Republica Italiana) by Prime Minister Silvio Berlusconi for services to Italian wine

2006
Elin McCoy writes a biography, *The Emperor of Wine: The rise of Robert M. Parker, Jr., and the reign of American taste*

2011
Receives the Gran Cruz de la Orden del Mérito Civil), Spain's highest civic honor, from King Juan Carlos of Spain

2012
Appoints Lisa Perrotti-Brown as *The Wine Advocate*'s new editor-in-chief and sells his majority stake in the business to Singapore investors for $15 million

ROBERT M. PARKER, JR.

From the late 1980s, American wine critic Robert Parker dominated professional commentary on the world's most sought-after wines. Founder of the bimonthly review *The Wine Advocate*, he is also the author of several acclaimed books. He is known to prefer wines made in a ripe-tasting, opulent style and his pronouncements hold huge sway, especially with wine collectors.

Robert Parker grew up in rural Maryland. With no formal training in wine, his interest was sparked in 1967, while visiting the French region of Alsace. From then on, he started tasting wines eagerly and continued tasting widely and writing notes while studying law at the University of Maryland.

Back in the 1970s, independent, impartial opinion on wine quality was not always easy to find, so in 1978, inspired by consumer activist Ralph Nader, Parker began publishing his own. Accepting no advertising, he vowed not be influenced by vested interests, history, or tradition. His early, unconditional praise for Bordeaux's 1982 vintage, when others were more cautious, proved to be a huge turning point and slowly but surely raised his profile considerably at home and abroad. In 1984, he retired from law and worked long hours assessing up to 10,000 wines a year at the peak of his career.

Robert Parker is perhaps best known for his 100-point wine rating scale, which, he maintains, permits "rapid communication of information to expert and novice alike." Top marks can instantly raise demand for, and the price of, individual wines and Parker points®, as they are known, are now routinely used as a promotional tool by wine trade professionals.

Critics of this system include British wine writer Hugh Johnson, who posits that wine does not lend itself to such rigid numeric assessment. Others claim that some producers actively target high scores by altering their wines to appeal to Parker's tastes, a phenomenon referred to as the "Parkerization" of wine.

Although Robert Parker may divide opinion, it is widely accepted that he has made fine wine more accessible to a new generation of consumers. In recognition of his services, he has received some of the highest civic honors from the governments of France, Italy, and Spain.

In 2006, he began delegating the coverage of various wine regions to trusted members of his staff—although he remains active, continuing to insure his nose in 2008 for $1 million—only relinquishing editorial control in 2012.

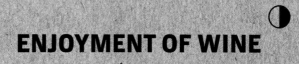

ENJOYMENT OF WINE

balance The overall harmony brought by the flavor and textural elements of a wine. A sweet wine requires acidity, a tannic red, a certain amount of ripe fruit. If any one element stands out, such as excessive alcohol or searing acidity, a wine is deemed to be unbalanced.

blind tasting An objective form of wine tasting in which participants assess the quality of a wine, and in some instances try to determine its precise origin without knowing its identity. Its prime benefit is to eliminate prejudices surrounding price, name, and region.

cork taint A wine fault caused by a cork contaminated with trichloranisole (TCA), which causes the wine to smell moldy and stale. It develops during manufacture as a result of cork bark being treated with a chlorine solution, which reacts with the phenolics in the cork. In recent years, new processes have reduced the incidence of taint, which at its height was thought to have affected around 1 in 20 bottles.

dry A technical term that denotes a wine with little or no residual grape sugar. Often a wine has a ripe fruit flavor that suggests a degree of sweetness despite it being technically dry.

The French Paradox A term coined in the United States in 1991, in an attempt to explain statistical evidence that the French recorded a comparatively low incidence of coronary heart disease despite consuming larger quantities of saturated fats and units of alcohol per capita than most other nationalities. Red wine was cited as a possible influencing factor.

horizontal tasting A tasting of a number of wines from the same vintage, usually for purposes of comparison. By contrast, a **vertical tasting** is a tasting of different vintages of the same wine, usually also for purposes of comparison.

residual sugar The amount of grape sugar left in a wine after fermentation. Anything less than 3 grams per liter will taste completely dry.

table wine The internationally accepted term to describe still wines of average alcoholic strength (9–15 degrees by volume) as distinct from fortified wines. Table wines derive their alcohol naturally during fermentation, while fortified wines have been strengthened by the addition of a neutral-tasting alcoholic spirit. Within the European Union, however, table wine has additional connotations, being the most generic and undemanding quality wine category. Table wine translates as follows: France, *vin de table*, Italy, *vino da tavola*; Spain, *vino de mesa*, Portugal, *vinho de mesa*, Germany, *tafelwein*.

TASTING TERMS

Words that form part of the wine taster's lexicon that help describe the characteristic color, aroma, and taste of a wine. While many words are immediately and universally understood, others pertain specifically to wine tasting and cannot, therefore, be taken literally. Here are some of the more common tasting terms that may require explanation.

APPEARANCE

core The center of a glass of wine when held and tilted away from the taster.

rim The pale, sometimes watery-looking edge of a glass of wine when held and tilted away from the taster.

legs/tears The transparent strands of alcohol that run down the sides of a glass after swirling it or drinking from it. The higher the wine's alcoholic strength, the more noticeable the legs.

mousse A French term used to describe the fizziness of a freshly poured glass of sparkling wine.

SMELL

aroma An individual scent, such as berries or vanilla, that forms part of a wine's overall bouquet.

bouquet The sum total of a wine's aromas.

clean The aroma of a wine with no obvious faults.

TASTE

attack The first impression a wine makes upon entering the mouth.

length The amount of time the flavor of a wine persists on the palate after swallowing or spitting.

finish The final impression left by a wine after swallowing or spitting. Often qualified by words such as "smooth," "long," "persistent," "aromatic," or "dry."

AGING WINE

Wines are typically aged for two reasons: to wait for the perfect drinking window and/or to appreciate in value. Wines bought for investment will maintain their best possible price if kept in professional storage facilities, because the correct storage environment is crucial for controlling maturation. Key criteria include: a dark place to protect the wine from ultraviolet rays, constant temperature (preferably 50–57.2°F/10–14°C), humidity (ideally 50–70 per cent), and laying bottles horizontally, to make sure the corks do not dry out. The least common style to be aged are dry white table wines, being lighter in structure, although those made from Chardonnay, Chenin Blanc, Riesling, and Semillon are capable of long life. Top-quality dessert wines that are high in sugar, such as Tokaji and Sauternes, can age for decades. Fortified wines also possess the structure to age magnificently, especially port and even more so Madeira, which can keep for a century or more. Dry red table wines, made from grapes with abundant acidity and high levels of tannin, provide the framework for successful aging, although maturation in oak barrels also contributes to higher tannins. Some of the world's most revered reds require patience: Bordeaux, Burgundy, Rioja, Napa Cabernet Sauvignon, the Super Tuscans, and Barolo.

RELATED TOPICS

See also
SWEET WINES
page 42

FORTIFIED WINES
page 44

ÉLEVAGE
page 46

EXPERT
Jane Parkinson

3-SECOND SIP

Good wine is worth keeping and great wine is built to last; it pays to store it well and reap the rewards when it reaches its peak condition.

3-MINUTE TOP OFF

In the last 25 years, Sotheby's have conducted four auctions of wines recovered from a famous collection of wines once owned by Nicholas II, the last czar of Russia, from the Massandra Winery at Yalta on Ukraine's Black Sea coast. Preserved in deep tunnels in Crimea under Stalin's orders, hundreds of bottles survived, some more than 150 years old, and included Madeiras, ports, and locally produced Muscats.

Many fine wines are built to last and, unlike most perishable goods, improve in quality over years or decades, if the conditions are right.

HOW TO TASTE

Wine is usually consumed without being subject to scrutiny, but professionals—winemakers, sommeliers, buyers, and journalists—and enthusiastic amateurs take an analytical approach to wine through the process of tasting, which begins with sight. A wine can be clear or cloudy (not necessarily a fault because unfiltered wine can be cloudy and perfectly fine); its color hints at both grape variety and age; while the "legs" indicate a high sugar and/or alcohol content. On the bouquet, the most common fault is cork taint—caused by a biological reaction between the wine and mold inside the cork. Recognizable aromas and flavors on the nose and palate can imply grape variety, oak, and the wine's origin. A mouth-puckering effect—the result of a wine with high acidity—can suggest cool climates, grapes that have been picked early, and/or grapes naturally high in acidity. Sweetness comes in varying degrees, from none for dry wines to intensely luscious for supersweet wines, while tannin—the sometimes textured mouthfeel—commonly derives from contact with the grape skins during fermentation and possibly with oak during maturation (if wine is aged in new oak). Before tasting, professionals avoid anything that can weaken their palate—coffee, chocolate, or toothpaste—or overpower a wine's delicate aroma—such as wearing perfume or aftershave.

3-SECOND SIP
Professional tasters undertake a sensory evaluation of a wine based on appearance, aroma, flavor, body, complexity, finish, and overall quality.

3-MINUTE TOP OFF
"Vertical" is the name given to a tasting that comprises the same wine from a range of vintages, whereas "horizontal" refers to a tasting of different wines from the same vintage. "Blind" tasting is the most intense form of tasting and involves providing no information about the wine, including covering its label.

RELATED TOPICS
See also
CLOSURES
page 48

AGING WINE
page 144

3-SECOND BIOGRAPHY
MAXIMILIAN RIEDEL
1977–
Eleventh-generation member of the Austrian family that has manufactured crystal wine glasses since 1756

EXPERT
Jane Parkinson

Tasting determines the various facets of a wine's character and is far more than a simple "Do I like this?" test.

WINE & FOOD

3-SECOND SIP
Choosing similar styles of wine and food and balancing their complementary flavors are among the best ways to ensure a harmonious match.

3-MINUTE TOP OFF
Because the countries of origin of spicy foods often do not have a wine-drinking culture, matching remains a work in progress. However, aromatic, fruity, and low-alcohol wines consistently prove themselves to work well with spice, while wines that are high in tannin or alcohol are best avoided.

Matching wine and food is subjective to some degree. However, a few practical guidelines are worth keeping in mind to avoid any clash of combinations. Pairing rich food with rich wine, for example, is one useful method to follow. Conversely, contrasting wine and food can provide excellent results, such as light crisp white wine to cut through oily fish. One easily understood principle is to match food with wine from the same area, because generations of association with local produce reveal natural affinities between regional specialities. Common sense is often all that need apply. Rich meaty dishes are always going to be natural partners for bold reds, such as Barolo or Shiraz, or pink seafood with dry rosé. Pinot Noir, incidentally—and usefully—is one of the most versatile food-matching grapes around. Cheese is a minefield, because there are so many different types. Historically, red wine was favored, but today white is increasingly served with some cheeses, because its inherent freshness counteracts the high fat content. Here, too, there are regional precedents, such as chalky goat cheese with crisp Sauvignon Blanc, both products of Sancerre on the Loire, or Comté cheese from the limestone hills of the Jura with *vin jaune*, the local speciality made from the Savagnin grape grown in this region of eastern France.

RELATED TOPICS
See also
REGIONAL GRAPES & WINE STYLES
page 74

SOMMELIERS
page 132

EXPERT
Jane Parkinson

Enjoying wine with food is a matter of personal preference and taste, but some flavors and styles definitely bring out the best in each other.

April 13 1902
Born George Philippe de
Rothschild in Paris

1922
Placed in charge of
Château Mouton
Rothschild

1924
Decrees that all wine
should be Château-
bottled, and commissions
a label by artist Jean
Carlu featuring the words
"mise en bouteille au
Château"

1926
Builds the spectacular,
Charles Siclis-designed
Grand Chai

1929
Racing his own Bugatti
T35C, he comes fourth in
the Monaco Grand Prix

1930
Creates Mouton Cadet
to market wine deemed
of insufficient quality
for an official Mouton
Rothschild vintage

1932
Produces the movie
Lac-aux-Dames, the first
French "talkie" to achieve
international recognition

1933
Establishes the wine
négociant business,
Baron Philippe de
Rothschild SA in Pauillac

1933
Purchases Fifth Growth
Château Mouton
d'Armailhacq (renamed
Château d'Armailhac in 1989)

1934
Marries Elisabeth
Pelletier de Chambure

1941
Joins the Free French
Forces of General Charles
de Gaulle, later earning a
Croix de Guerre medal

1945
Commissions original
label artwork from
Philippe Jullian to
commemorate the allied
victory; the wine label
has featured original
artwork every year since

1954
Marries his mistress
Pauline Fairfax Potter

1962
Opens the Museum of
Wine in Art

1970
Purchases the
neighboring Fifth Growth
Château Clerc Milon

1973
Mouton is elevated to
Premier Cru Classé status,
following a decree signed
by Jacques Chirac,
Minister of Agriculture

1979
Creates Opus One with
California's Robert
Mondavi, the first
Franco-Californian
ultrapremium wine,
"planted, made, matured,
and blended in the
traditional Bordeaux
manner"

January 20 1988
Dies in Bordeaux at the
age of 85

BARON PHILIPPE DE ROTHSCHILD

Grand Prix racing driver, French freedom fighter, movie producer, art collector, poet, playwright, and playboy, Baron Philippe de Rothschild was a universal man. Above all, however, he was the protagonist in the story of Bordeaux wine in the twentieth century.

In 1922, the young Baron was put in charge of his family's wine property, Château Mouton Rothschild, where he had spent many happy years as a teenager during World War I. It had always rankled him that in Bordeaux's famous 1855 Classification, Mouton had not been deemed a Premier Cru, or "First Growth," when the market price suggested it should have been. He vowed one day he would overturn this "injustice."

In the 1920s, it was still common practice for wines to be shipped in barrel and bottled abroad. Unscrupulous merchants would sometimes "stretch" supplies of great wine by blending them with *vin ordinaire*. Baron Philippe deemed that vintages should be bottled at the Château in order to guarantee quality and authenticity. Other estates soon followed suit.

The move also presented marketing opportunities. For the 1924 vintage, he commissioned graphic artist Jean Carlu to design an art deco label, sending shock waves through conservative Bordeaux. The daring concept was relaunched in 1945, and original, individual labels have been the Mouton signature ever since. Artists include Dalí (1958), Miró (1969), Chagall (1970), Picasso (1973), Warhol (1975), Prince Charles (2004), and Xu Lei (2008).

To maintain impeccable standards, Baron Philippe did not release the disappointing 1930 vintage as Mouton Rothschild but as a brand he created and named Mouton Cadet. Over time, sourced from various Bordeaux vineyards, it became the region's biggest seller.

In 1962, he opened the world-class Museum of Art in Wine in the estate's former barrel hall, but the Baron's crowning achievement came in 1973. After forty years of tireless campaigning, Mouton Rothschild was elevated to Premier Cru Classé. This caused much consternation among the Bordeaux establishment. No change to the sacrosanct 1855 classification has been made since, and it is highly probable it never will be changed again.

In 1979, recognizing the great potential of New World wines, he embarked on a joint venture with California's Robert Mondavi, launching the Napa Valley's first superpremium wine, Opus One. Right up until his death in 1988, Baron Philippe remained a maverick and trendsetter, one of the most influential figures in wine, in Bordeaux and beyond.

WINE & HEALTH

RELATED TOPICS
See also
SULFUR DIOXIDE
page 34

MAKING RED WINE
page 38

EXPERT
Jane Parkinson

3-SECOND SIP
Drunk in moderation, red wine is widely believed to be the most beneficial wine style for one's health, because of its high level of antioxidants.

Wine and health is no modern issue, dating back as far as ancient Greece with the physician Hippocrates famous for believing wine to be an integral part of a healthy diet. Today, reports on the benefits or perils of drinking wine are endlessly debated, and although some are dismissed more quickly than others, one of the most enduring dates from the late twentieth century. The French Paradox observed the low incidence of coronary heart disease among people living in the south of France despite their notoriously rich diet, leading researchers to suggest red wine was the cause of this anomaly. Red wine is often cited as the most health-inducing style of wine, because it is high in anthocyanins, which contain powerful antioxidants. One of these, resveratrol, occurs in grape skins and vine leaves, and because red wine production typically involves longer contact of the juice with the skins, more resveratrol is extracted in making red wine than white. It's a widely held belief that the darker a wine's color, the higher its antioxidant content, although some authorities consider climate to be important in determining the levels of resveratrol in a grape, suggesting that grapes from cool, wet regions contain higher levels of resveratrol than those from hot and arid conditions.

3-MINUTE TOP OFF
Governments around the globe are under constant pressure to warn the public of the health effects of alcohol. Many release advice on how frequently it is drunk and the quantity that should be drunk, fervently supporting moderate consumption, because bingedrinking is considered harmful to health. Despite its wine-drinking culture, France has one of the harshest laws, la Loi Evin, restricting the advertising of alcohol.

The benefits, or otherwise, of the amount and type of wine we drink continues to generate healthy debate and discussion; the antioxidant resveratrol is found in the skin of grapes, and its benefits continue to be studied.

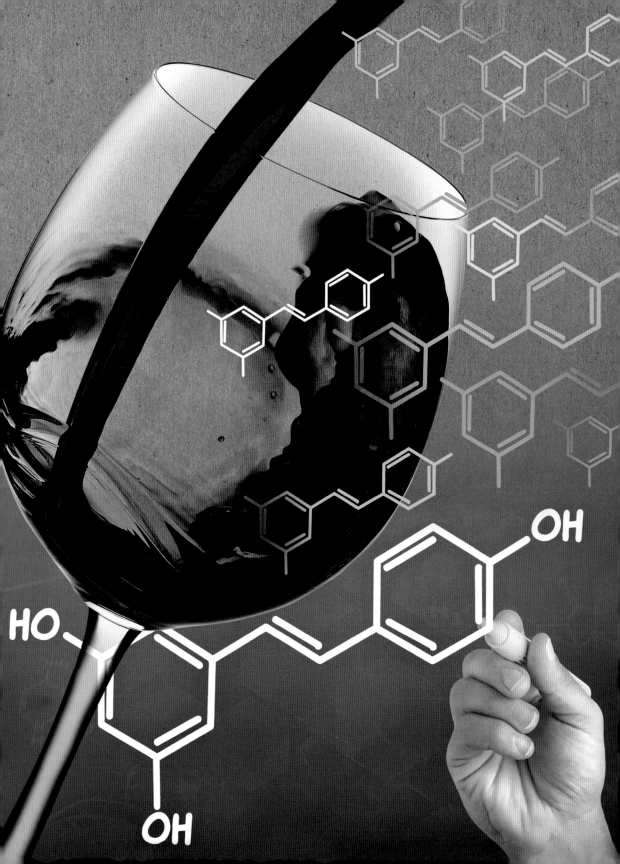

RESOURCES

BOOKS

Best White Wine on Earth:
The Riesling Story
Stuart Pigott
(Stewart, Tabori & Chang, 2011)

Bordeaux Legends
Jane Anson
(Stewart, Tabori & Chang, 2013)

The Grapevine: From the Science to the Practice
of Growing Grapes for Wine
Patrick Iland, Peter R. Dry & Tony Proffitt
(Patrick Iland Wine Promotions, 2011)

Inside Burgundy
Jasper Morris
(2010)

Inventing Wine: A New History
of One of the World's Most
Ancient Pleasures
Paul Lukacs
(W. W. Norton & Co., 2013)

Riesling Renaissance
Freddy Price
(Mitchell Beazley, 2004)

The Story of Wine
Hugh Johnson
(Mitchell Beazley, 2004)

Understanding Wine Technology
David Bird
(BBQA Publishing, 2010)

Venture into Viticulture.
Tom Crossen
(Country Wide Press, 2003)

Vintage: The Story of Wine
Hugh Johnson
(Simon & Schuster, 1989)

Viticulture: An introduction
to Commercial Grape Growing
for Wine Production
Stephen Skelton MW
(S. P. Skelton, 2009)

Viticulture Volume 1: Resources
B. G. Coombe & P. R. Dry (eds)
(Winetitles, 1998)

Viticulture Volume 2: Practices
B. G. Coombe & P. R. Dry (eds)
(Winetitles, 2006)

*Wine Science: The Application
of Science in Winemaking*
Jamie Goode
(Mitchell Beazley, 2014)

The World Atlas of Wine
Hugh Johnson & Jancis Robinson
(Mitchell Beazley, 2013)

Yquem
Richard Olney
(Flammarion, 2007)

MAGAZINES/JOURNALS

Decanter
decanter.com

Wine Spectator
winespectator.com

The World of Fine Wine
worldoffinewine.com

WEBSITES

Jancis Robinson's Purple Pages
jancisrobinson.com

Food & Wine
foodandwine.com

wine.com

NOTES ON CONTRIBUTORS

CONSULTANT EDITOR
Gérard Basset OBE is currently the only person in the world to be given the combined titles of Master of Wine, Master Sommelier, Wine MBA, and the World's Best Sommelier. Trained in Lyon, he became head sommelier at a Michelin-starred hotel in England and went on to cofound the Hôtel du Vin chain. Basset was honored with the OBE (an honor awarded by the British monarch) in 2011 for services to the hospitality industry and named Man of the Year by *Decanter* magazine in 2013.

FOREWORD
Annette Alvarez-Peters is the principal buyer and director of wine for Costco, the sixth largest retailer in the United States.

CONTRIBUTORS
David Bird MW trained as an analytical chemist and entered the food manufacturing business as an analyst working with baby foods, mustard, and fruit-flavored beverages. He moved into the wine trade in 1973, almost by chance, but in reality because a passion for wine was already developing. His vintage year was 1981, when he became a Master of Wine, a Chartered Chemist, and father to his first son. He specializes in quality assurance techniques, such as ISO 9000 and Hazard Analysis, and has been involved with wine activities in France, Italy, Spain, Portugal, Hungary, Denmark, Ukraine, Russia, Algeria, Australia, and England.

Martin Campion has spent twenty-five years in the wine trade, working for Laithwaite's Wine and its sister companies. He is a passionate advocate for fine German Riesling, visiting many of the country's top producers every spring to taste the new vintage and attending the VDP's September auctions, where most of the finest and rarest wines are sold. He lectures on Laithwaite's Wine and Spirits Education Trust program and judges at the Decanter World Wine Awards, the International Wine Challenge, and Meininger's Best of Riesling in Germany.

Jeremy Dixon first studied wine with the Australian Wine and Brandy Corporation in the 1980s before heading overseas to complete the WSET Diploma in London and the D.U.A.D at Bordeaux University's Institut d'Oenologie. His hands-on experience includes nine vintages as assistant winemaker in Theizé, Beaujolais. Today, a freelance commercial writer, he specializes in wine, food, and travel for clients such as the Telegraph Group; he works extensively for Laithwaite's and judges on occasions at the Decanter World Wine Awards.

Paul Lukacs is a professor of English at Loyola University, Maryland, and a wine writer with a special interest in wine history. A wine columnist in Washington, DC, for nearly twenty years, he has won numerous awards for his work, and his books include *American Vintage: The Rise of American Wine* and *Inventing Wine: A New*

History of One of the World's Most Ancient Pleasures.

Debra Meiburg ᴍᴡ is an award-winning author, TV personality, international speaker, and a leading voice in wine education in Greater China. She was ranked the seventh most powerful woman in wine by the *Drinks Business* magazine. Debra is producer and host of several documentaries and TV shows, including *Taste the Wine*, which is broadcast in twenty-six countries. She developed a suite of award-winning wine educational books and tools currently distributed on four continents, as well as guides to the Hong Kong, Shanghai, Beijing, and Singapore Wine Trades, firmly establishing her as a key voice for wine in Asia.

Jane Parkinson is an award-winning wine journalist and broadcaster. Recently awarded the International Wine & Spirit Competition Communicator of the Year 2014 title, she is a wine expert on BBC1 *Saturday Kitchen Live* and released her debut book *Wine & Food* in 2014. Jane is Wine Editor of *Restaurant* magazine, Wine Expert for *Stylist* magazine, and one of five members of The Wine Gang. She regularly contributes to magazines and newspapers and discusses wine on radio and television. Jane is also a previous recipient of the Chairman's Award at the Louis Roederer International Wine Writers' Awards.

Stephen Skelton ᴍᴡ started his career in wine in 1975. After twelve months at Schloss Schönborn in Germany's Rheingau wine-growing region and two terms at Geisenheim Wine School, he returned to the UK in 1977 to establish Tenterden Vineyards in Kent (now the home of the UK's largest wine producer Chapel Down), where he made wine for twenty-three vintages. He was also winemaker at Lamberhurst Vineyards between 1988 and 1991. He became a Master of Wine in 2003, and won the prestigious Mondavi Prize. In 2005, he was awarded the AXA Millésimes award for his contribution to the work of the MW Education Committee. In 2014, he was elected to be Deputy Vice Chairman of the Institute of Masters of Wine. He also lectures on viticulture for Wine and Spirit Education Trust's Diploma courses. Stephen is a consultant to the English wine industry and is involved with planting vineyards for the production of both regular and sparkling wines. Since 1986, he has written and lectured widely on English wine and has published four guides to UK vineyards, the 2001 edition of which won the André Simon award for "Wine Book of the Year." He has also written *Viticulture*, a primer on the subject for students, and *Wine Growing in Great Britain* for growers.

INDEX

ACKNOWLEDGMENTS

PICTURE CREDITS
The publisher would like to thank the following individuals and organizations for permission to reproduce copyright material:

All images from Shutterstock, Inc./www.shutterstock.com and Clipart Images/www.clipart.com unless stated.

21: Jamie Bush.
22: Ivan Hissey.
27b: Tyson Kopfer/Cayuse Vineyards.
33: Dr. Jeremy Burgess/Science Photo Library.
41t: Eric Zeziola/Champagne Louis Roederer.
41b: Lordprice Collection/Alamy.
43t: Bon Appetit/Alamy.
43b: Craig Hatfield.
45tl: Gonzalez Byass.
45tr: Thomas Istvan Seibel.
46: Kirsten Georgi.
50: Roux Olivier/Sagaphoto.com /Alamy.
68: Lacy Atkins/San Francisco Chronicle/Corbis.
85r: Philippe Roy/Hemis/Corbis.
85l: Interfoto/Sammlung Rauch/Mary Evans.
93tr: Champagne/Alamy.
94: Nik wheeler/Alamy.
103: Stephanie Evans.
107: Library of Congress.
118: Bloomberg/Contributor.
121t: Clay McLachlan/Aurora Photos.
121r: Lou Linwei/Alamy.
129: Peter Wheeler/Alamy.
132: Alamy/Ian Shaw; OJO Images; Robert Kneschke.
135: Raymond Reuter/Sygma/Corbis.
138: Patrick Bernard/Stringer.
150: Charles O'Rear/Corbis.

All reasonable efforts have been made to trace copyright holders and to obtain their permission for the use of copyright material. The publisher apologizes for any errors or omissions in the list above and will gratefully incorporate any corrections in future reprints if notified.